Contents

D1434972

Understanding and **Supporting**
Refugee Children and **Young People:**
A Practical Resource for Teachers, Parents and
Carers of Those Exposed to the Trauma of War

Contents

Understanding and Supporting Refugee Children and Young People:
A Practical Resource for Teachers, Parents and Carers of Those Exposed to the Trauma of War

Contents

Foreword

This book is the **go-to resource** for those parents and professionals seeking to support children through the trauma of war and conflict. Not only does it provide the evidence base for effectively integrating refugee children into their new schools, but it also introduces the reader to a range of key tools and strategies to both understand and manage anxiety and trauma-related behaviours. Practical and user-friendly, it demystifies the process of talking about difficult topics, providing helpful advice on how to do this in a trauma-informed way, making use of effective tools from therapeutic approaches to help our children and ourselves remain regulated and able to engage in post-traumatic growth.

About the author

Dr Tina Rae has 40 years' experience working with children, adults, and families in clinical and educational contexts within local authorities and specialist services. She is currently working as a Consultant Educational and Child Psychologist in a range of SEMH and mainstream contexts and is a widely published author.

Recent publications include the following:

- Rae, T. *(2022)* **The Bereavement Book: Activities to Support Children** and **Young People through grief** and **loss.**
  Buckingham: Hinton House Publishers
- Rae, T. & D'Amario, A. *(2021)* **A Recovery Toolbox** of **Wellbeing in the Early years** for **children aged 3-6.**
  Buckingham: Hinton House Publishers
- Rae, T. & D'Amario, A. *(2021)* **A Recovery Toolbox** of **Wellbeing** for **Primary Aged Children 7-11.**
  Buckingham: Hinton House Publishers
- Rae, T. & D'Amario, A. *(2021)* **A Recovery Toolbox** of **Wellbeing** for **Adolescents** and **Teenagers aged 12-16.**
  Buckingham: Hinton House Publishers
- Rae, T. *(2021)* **My Toolbox** of **Wellbeing Journal** – **creative, inspiring activities** and **strategies.**
  Buckingham: Hinton House Publishers
- Rae, T. *(2020)* **Supporting Children** and **Young People** with **Emotionally Based School Avoidance.**
  Buckingham: Hinton House Publishers
- Rae, T. Middleton, T. & Walshe, J. *(2020)* **Nurturing Peer Supervision: Supporting** the **Wellbeing of those who Nurture.**
  Glasgow: Nurture UK
- Rae, T. *(2020)* **It's OK not to be OK: A Guide to Wellbeing.**
  London: QED Publishing
- Rae, T. *(2020)* **A Toolbox of Wellbeing: Helpful strategies** and **activities** for **Children, Teens,** their **Carers** and **Teachers.**
  Buckingham: Hinton House Publishers
- Rae, T. Such, A. & Wood, J. *(2020)* **The Well Being Tool Kit** for **Mental health leads** in **schools, A comprehensive Training Resource** to **Support Emotional Wellbeing** in **Education** and **Social Care.**
  Buckingham: Hinton House Publishers

Introduction

As I write this introduction, the war in Ukraine continues to affect us all on an ongoing basis. During my 40-year career to date, I have never been as inundated with requests for psychological support and help from both parents, professionals and children and young people regarding heightened levels of anxiety, trauma-related behaviours and symptoms and significant mental health needs. In a time when access to specialist therapeutic services remains problematic and resources incredibly limited, it is more important than ever that we can access evidence-based and practical tools to support us in managing our own wellbeing and that of the children and young people we nurture and love.

All of us who work in the education or psychology disciplines recognise the extent to which many children and young people are experiencing an erosion in their mental health and wellbeing. For some, this is clearly linked to the Covid pandemic and the uncertainty and anxiety it has brought to all our lives. The Institute of Fiscal Studies *(Banks & Xiaowei, 2020)* has reported an 8.7% decline in wellbeing, and NHS monitoring is currently observing spikes in self-harm and eating disorders which are occurring in children younger than previously identified. Recent research from Cardiff University *(Moore & Morgan, 2021)* has also indicated that the impact of the pandemic will leave a '***lifelong footprint***' on the mental health of this generation of children.

Psychological services, both private and public sector, are currently inundated with requests for advice and intervention. Alongside the ongoing trauma of the Covid pandemic and the increase in mental health difficulties in our children and young people as a direct result of lockdowns, reduced access to social contexts, missed educational opportunities and rites of passage, our young people are now also experiencing heightened levels of stress as they seek to navigate the reality of war. It is as if the collective trauma has been doubled within a very short space of time.

Added to this, we are now currently navigating the arrival and transition of thousands of refugee children and young people into our country and into our educational system.

It is therefore imperative that appropriate support is provided to those who exhibit the symptoms of anxiety and trauma and also to whole school communities in order to both build and maintain a Recovery curriculum and whole school systems to promote wellbeing. At the heart of this, of course, are the teachers and support staff who are tasked with such an objective within underfunded and under resourced-communities – despite recent DfE initiatives *(2022)*.

From my perspective, as an educational and child psychologist, there is a great deal that we can now do in terms of ensuring we effectively support our children to navigate the stressful times and also to successfully integrate our refugee children into nurturing, trauma-informed classrooms and schools of sanctuary.

This is my rationale for producing this resource. I am hoping that it will provide parents, carers and professionals with practical, user-friendly advice and

Understanding and Supporting
Refugee Children and Young People:
A Practical Resource for Teachers, Parents and Carers of Those Exposed to the Trauma of War

resources to support our children and young people in talking about, understanding, and processing war and conflict alongside effectively managing their anxiety and fears. I am also hoping that the resource will also clarify how best to support our refugee children and young people and their carers and school-based staff and professionals who are seeking to create safe havens and deliver practical interventions to promote post-traumatic growth.

In a time when many adults are feeling overwhelmed and have so many questions about how to support their children, there is clearly a need for accessible resources which do not compound a sense of helplessness but rather provides genuine hope they can and should be able to effectively navigate this situation, recognising and developing the skills they need to maintain self-regulation and can regulate with their children and young people. This has never been more important in my view.

'We know that unregulated and stressed adults cannot effectively support and help children and young people who are also unregulated and stressed. It is impossible.'
(Rae, 2020, p7)

The **first social media war**

It is important to note that a significant factor in the levels of stress that we are all experiencing in this time of trauma is the fact that this current war is unfolding in real time through a screen. We are consistently bombarded with images of destruction, people hiding in shelters and civilians saying their goodbyes to those that they love. There are so many disturbing and tragic events, and these are overwhelming and extremely difficult to process.

It is not only the fact that the war is being broadcast live on 24-hour TV, but it is also presented on social media via apps such as Instagram, Twitter, and tick-tock. Adults and many of our children and young people are viewing violent images on a daily basis and some of those videos which have been tagged *#Ukrainewar* have been viewed over 600 million times in a matter of days. Clearly, such material can be triggering to all of us and have a significant psychological impact.

Of course, the Ukraine war is one of many recent global conflicts. Unrest in Syria, the war in Afghanistan and instability in Iraq for example, and the worldwide Covid 19 pandemic are only a few of the items on a long list of traumatic events that have impacted on mental health across the globe.

War and mental health

The World Health Organisation *(WHO)(Srinivasa Murthy, & Lakshminarayana, (2006)* has stated that in situations of armed conflict, approximately 10% of those who experience traumatic events will subsequently develop a serious mental health problem. A further 10% will also develop behaviour which prevents them from functioning effectively on a day-to-day basis. The most common effects are depression, anxiety, and psychosomatic problems such as insomnia. **They further identify three populations who will be susceptible to negative mental health outcomes:**

- ■ **Civilians** *(including children)* **within the targeted homeland**
- ■ **The soldiers on both sides of the conflict**
- ■ **Those consuming the images, videos and audio of the war through social media apps television, radio, and the web**

All three groups, including civilians may develop the typical psychological profile of trauma. They may also develop a deep suspicion, a sense of mistrust and hopelessness regarding any conflict which is close to home or far away.

From a clinical perspective, when it comes to times of crisis, more people now turn to electronic media as sources of information. Many individuals use social media to cope with stress or as a distraction. Watching the events across Ukraine and the rest of the world unfold on a screen allows them to empathise with those who are affected and can educate, inform, and inspire people to help. But increased screen time and oversaturation of traumatic content can also come at a significant cost to mental health overall.

So, it is vital that we all recognise how we can and should turn off our screens or limit the time viewing content which is triggering and traumatic. We need to recognise how social media algorithms are purposely built to be addictive and seek actively to combat this by our own self-care routines and behaviours.

In my view, this is vital if we are to truly maintain our own wellbeing so that we are fit for purpose in terms of supporting our children and young people as they navigate war and conflict and engage in post-traumatic growth.

PAGE
4

Understanding and **Supporting**
Refugee Children and **Young People**:
A Practical Resource for Teachers, Parents and
Carers of Those Exposed to the Trauma of War

I think that there are FOUR KEYS to doing this successfully:

1. DEVELOP AN UNDERSTANDING OF TRAUMA AND ANXIETY

It is important to remember and understand how chronic stress, and the effects of trauma and anxiety impact on our thinking. This can then help us to support children more effectively in terms of making the right kinds of adjustments to the learning context and in relating more therapeutically with individuals exhibiting such difficulties.

Children and young people may exhibit the following symptoms:

- **Poor concentration**
- **less reliable working memory**
- **problems in organising and prioritising their work or activities**

It is therefore vital that all involved in supporting them take care to allow additional time to process information and to support them with maintaining organisational skills with a range of tools including personalised checklists, visual timetables, and breaking tasks into smaller more manageable chunks.

Children can also become **hypervigilant and focus on only the negative outcomes, underestimating their ability to cope.**

This can lead to a loss of confidence and lowering of self-esteem overall. They may also engage in more black-and-white thinking where they think that everything will always be bad or always go wrong. Making such assumptions can lead to a **cycle of negative thinking, feeling, and behaving alongside distortion of their own perceptions**. Again, it is particularly important to understand these key factors and how to support the child or young person in gently challenging such negative patterns of thinking, feeling, and behaving.

It is also important to understand that **anxiety very often exhibits itself as anger and embarrassment**. They are merely displaying the symptoms of their anxiety. It is therefore vital that the child or young person is supported on an emotional level and not punished for displaying such symptoms. This more nuanced and appropriate response can be also further supported through the development of trauma-informed classrooms and safe spaces.

Increased school avoidance

Anxious feelings about school

Decrease in motivation

Falling behind in school work

Pleasurable activities at home

Loss of friends and increased isolation

Increased anxiety around school

Immediate anxiety reduces

Negative thoughts about school and one's ability to cope

Avoid the situation that is invoking the anxiety

2. DEVELOP AN UNDERSTANDING OF HOW TO CREATE TRAUMA-INFORMED CLASSROOMS AND SAFE SPACES

The trauma-informed classroom ensures that all children can feel safe, nurtured, and included.

There are **SIX** key areas we can focus on right now:

1. **Belonging** - *making sure the children feel welcomed, wanted and part of the group*

2. **Predictability** - *making sure that changes to routines are explained clearly and with empathy*

3. **Organisation** - *ensuring that the routines and activities are consistent and visual checklists are provided as necessary*

4. **Regulation** - *teaching an emotional literacy curriculum and ensuring a safe space or calm corner is available to children and young people and that they understand how to use this effectively in order to self-regulate*

5. **Differentiation** - *reduce processing demands in the classroom and provide clear structures or plans for each task*

6. **Relationships** - *keep connections healthy and empathic, modelling social skills and valuing and celebrating their strengths and achievements.*

PAGE
6

Understanding and **Supporting**
Refugee Children and **Young People:**
A Practical Resource for Teachers, Parents and
Carers of Those Exposed to the Trauma of War

3. DEVELOP AN UNDERSTANDING OF HOW TO USE SELF-REGULATION SKILLS AND STRATEGIES FROM KEY THERAPEUTIC APPROACHES SUCH AS CBT, POSITIVE PSYCHOLOGY AND MINDFULNESS

Self-regulation skills start to develop in early childhood. When children have experienced co-regulation through consistent, sensitive, and nurturing relationships, they begin to learn how to manage their own emotions. Neuroscientific research suggests that these relationships help to develop the links between the emotional limbic brain, and the cerebral cortex, allowing children to be better able to rationalise, reason, empathise and problem-solve.

Some calming techniques to model to them and to teach them to self-regulate include:

- Mindfulness
- Visualisation
- Grounding
- Sensory activities
- Controlled breathing

Mindfulness is a particularly useful and popular approach with the growing evidence base in terms of its use in schools *(Rae et al., 2017)*.

Making use of tools and positive psychology and cognitive behaviour therapy are also extremely effective in terms of supporting overall wellbeing.

These include:

- Challenging and reframing thoughts
- Engaging in positive self-talk
- Using affirmations
- Identifying three good things on a daily basis
- Expressing gratitude
- Journaling

It is important to note that supporting children and young people to make use of simple grounding techniques, mindful breathing exercises, visualisation and challenging negative automatic thoughts is something that **all adults** can undertake as long as they also take the time to make use of these strategies themselves and fully understand how to model them. This is all part of how they themselves can maintain their own wellbeing and provide good wellbeing role models to those they nurture and support in schools.

4. DEVELOP AN UNDERSTANDING OF HOW TO MAINTAIN SELF-CARE ROUTINES AND PEER SUPPORT FOR STAFF TEAMS

A final essential task for all who engage therapeutically or take on the role of the emotionally available adult is to look to ourselves first. We cannot pour from an empty cup.

The Healthy Mind Platter *(developed by Dr David Rock and Daniel J. Siegel)* has seven essential mental activities necessary for optimum mental health in daily life. At this point, it may well be worth considering *what you are doing to maintain wellbeing in these key areas in your life?* And what are the systems in your school or workplace which ensure staff wellbeing and mental health?

These questions need to be answered first before you begin to take on the role of the therapeutic adult who can successfully nurture our children and young people in these times of evident stress and anxiety.

I sincerely hope that subsequent chapters in this book will support you in this process. Alongside providing advice on how we talk to our children and young people about war and conflict, there are opportunities to gain an understanding of trauma, clarify and try out evidence-based strategies to support those with anxiety- and trauma-related behaviours, advice, and resources for supporting our refugee children, their parents and carers, and key tools and strategies from a range of therapeutic approaches from which we and our children and young people can all benefit.

This resource is presented in a user-friendly format, it is accessible and attempts to limit the use of any psychological or educational jargon. You will find practical ideas, tools, and strategies alongside a wealth of information and useful handouts and resources for young people and those who seek to support them in their journey of recovery and post-traumatic growth.

DOWN TIME **Let your mind wander.** Don't think about any particular goal.

FOCUS TIME **Closely focus on a task or goal.** This Challenge makes deep connections in the brain.

PLAY TIME **Sit back, relax, and be spontaneous!** Being creative and allowing time to *"just play"* helps the brain make new connections.

TIME IN **Shhhhh.** Quiet reflection helps to better integrate the brain. Focus on sensations, thoughts and feelings.

CONNECTING TIME **Connecting with others in person**, not via a screen! As well as stopping to connect.

PHYSICAL TIME **Get up get moving!** It strengthens the body, including the brain.

SLEEP TIME **Get your Zzzzz's!** While the brain snoozes, learning is consolidated. Sleep also allows the brain to recover from the day's experiences.

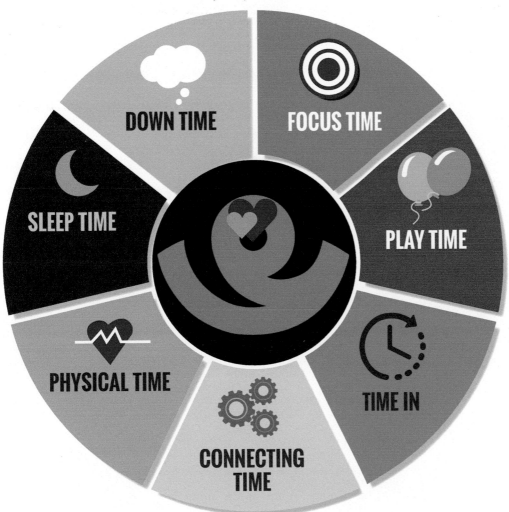

CHAPTER 1

Talking to children and young people about war and conflict

This chapter covers

- Talking about war plan
- The need for validation
- Using an emotion coaching approach
- The need to be a good listener
- Helpful phrases you could use in your conversations
- Key phrases you might consider using when talking about war
- The need for honesty and age-appropriate language
- The importance of fact checking
- The importance of curious conversations
- Be aware of the unique lived experience of each child
- Finding the helpers and positive action
- 5 Anxiety easy wins
- Reinforce their sense of safety
- Keep regulated as the supportive adult in the relationship

PAGE
10

Understanding and **Supporting**
Refugee Children and **Young People:**
A Practical Resource for Teachers, Parents and
Carers of Those Exposed to the Trauma of War

We know that when war or a conflict is in the news our children and young people can and do experience a wide range of emotions which can be overwhelming for many of them.

However, what is also apparent is the fact that trying to engage with them in an empathic way, remaining calm and providing them with a secure base, can also be a very difficult task for us as the adults.

Talking to our children and young people about war and conflict is clearly an essential task for us all, but it also poses many pitfalls in helping children make sense of what is happening in an age-appropriate way.

In order to support adults in this task, I developed my **Talking about war plan**.

This concise framework highlights the key tasks involved in talking about war to our children and attempts to demystify some of the anxieties that many of us may experience in this process. This plan is designed to be copied and distributed to parents, carers, therapeutic support workers and school staff in order to provide a quick and accessible guide which does not overwhelm the reader.

I think the plan itself is relatively straightforward and clear, but it is important to highlight some key pieces of advice in terms of talking to our children and young people about war and conflict.

Talking about war plan

Talking about the war in an age-appropriate way with our children is essential as communication is key to reducing the fear of the unknown and related anxiety

Accept, validate, and affirm their feelings, making sure that they understand these are all normal in a time of trauma

Look to yourself first, taking the time to engage in *appropriate self-care* as you cannot keep your calm without this level of self-nurture

Keep regulated so that you can effectively co-regulate with your child

Information is readily available, so *'fact check'* with your children making sure that they access accurate information via trusted channels

Notice those who may be more vulnerable or at risk - particularly those children who are refugees themselves - making sure to provide the additional time and trauma-informed care they may need

Get grounded throughout the day using deep breathing, visualisation, or whatever works for you

Autonomy reduces anxiety, so take control, of what you can control, such as your self-care routines and reducing social media

Build in daily flow activities for children (*AND YOURSELF*) and make sure these include play and creativity

Observe the helpers - in times of war and danger there will always be people who try to help, and noticing and celebrating these people can rebuild a sense of hope

Understand and share knowledge of reliable facts and highlight these as needed, not denying the situation exists - if we don't talk about it, children will become even more anxious

Take time away when you need it in order to gain a better balance - not denying the dangers but highlighting moments of joy, gratitude, and good things that we can all still have

Watch your language, making sure that it's factual and information is always presented in a balanced way - *'this may be scary but there is still hope and there are still good people in this world'*

Anxiety reducing easy wins need to be reinforced, such as structure, routines, exercise, and quality time together

Relationships heal and build hope! So be that *steady, calm, and reassuring adult*, gaining your energy from those who show compassion and fearlessness in this time of trauma - never forget there will always be helpers so look for them first and let them inspire you to do likewise.

Understanding and **Supporting**
Refugee Children and **Young People:**
A Practical Resource for Teachers, Parents and
Carers of Those Exposed to the Trauma of War

The **need** for **validation**

The plan makes explicit the need to validate the child's reactions and responses. It is clearly normal for us to all feel anxious and stressed when we consider the tragedy of war and the horrific impacts it has on so many. It can be tempting to minimise the whole situation or reassure children with throwaway comments such as '*it's not really something to be worried about*' or '*it is so far away that it can't hurt you*'.

This kind of dismissing of their emotional responses can be very damaging. It also creates more anxiety as children will be left with the feeling that there really is something very wrong happening if we totally shield them from it. It is almost like we are creating the elephant in the room.

Using an **emotion coaching approach** (*Gottman & Declaire, 1997*) is key here. This is not a therapeutic intervention but simply a way of communicating with a child or young person that is both nurturing and respectful and helps them to manage those big worries and emotions.

Key steps to emotion coaching are as follows:

Step 1	Step 2	Step 3	Step 4
Empathising and validating	**Labelling emotions**	**Setting limits**	**Continued – Problem solving**
' I see'… or	'Are you feeling…?'	' It's okay to feel	' Tell me what happened to make you feel this way?'
' I notice'…	' Is there anything else that you are feeling?'	_ _ _ _ _ _ _ _ _ _	' What can you do to solve this problem?'
' I hear…'	' I imagine that feels…'	but it's never okay to	' Can you remember feeling this way before and what you did?'
' I'm wondering…'	' It sounds to me like you feel	_ _ _ _ _ _ _ _ _ _	' How did you handle it last time?'
' Tell me about that…'	_ _ _ _ _ _ _ _ _ _	' Even when we are annoyed, we can't act in that way because it's not safe'	' What could you do differently next time you feel this way?'
' Are you saying that…'	because	' This isn't a safe place to be angry, let's go somewhere safe and then we can talk'	' Is there anyone that could help you with this?'
' It's okay to feel that way'	_ _ _ _ _ _ _ _ _ _		' Let's take a look at some different choices…'
' I would feel angry too if I felt something was unfair'	Is that right?'		
' It's normal to feel that way sometimes'	' How does that make you feel?'		

Ultimately,

if you really want to understand a child or young person, you have to be able to put yourself in their shoes and try to feel what they are feeling.

This kind of empathetic listening totally underpins the emotion coaching approach. We have to show empathy to our children before we can begin to develop or propose solutions with them or for them.

So, what does this kind of listening look like? Gottman & Declaire *(1997)* **suggest that empathetic listeners do the following:**

Once the child or young person feels understood you can then reassure them that the way they are feeling is okay. It is quite normal, and you are not dismissing it.

Use *their eyes to identify physical evidence of the child's emotions.*

Use *their hearts to feel what the child is feeling.*

Use *their imaginations to put themselves in the child's shoes to understand how they're feeling.*

Use *their eyes to identify physical evidence of the child's emotions.*

Use *words to reflect back what they hear, see, and imagine in a soothing, non-judgemental way. These words also help the child label the emotion.*

PAGE
14

Understanding and **Supporting**
Refugee Children and **Young People:**
A Practical Resource for Teachers, Parents and
Carers of Those Exposed to the Trauma of War

The **need** to be a **good listener**

We know that an active listening approach and conveying empathy can help calm the child or young person, it can help them feel understood and allow them to express their emotions honestly so that you can find out their needs and assist them appropriately.

When talking to a child or young person, the following may be helpful:

- Seek information about the situation or worry or fear so you know how to help.
- Reassure them that that they do not need to re-tell their story in detail unless they say they want to. Pay attention to tone of voice, body language, and establishing good eye contact.
- Listen carefully to what people say and clarify your understanding by repeating back or summarising what you hear they are trying to communicate.
- Demonstrate you are listening using nods, murmurs or encouragers such as 'oh?' *or* 'OK' *or* 'I understand' - respond without judging.
- Be sensitive and focused, effective communication with a distressed child does not require probing into their experience. Accept and support emotions.
- Use language that is simple, direct, and easy to understand, speak slowly and calmly; try not to use euphemisms; offer hope, have patience, and leave gaps for them to start.
- Exercise patience if people are confused or find it difficult to explain. Tell them it is OK if they do not want to talk or tell their story; *be respectful and compassionate.*

Helpful phrases you could use in **your conversations**
Reflecting their concerns and experiences

- *"I understand your feelings and lots of people are feeling similarly to you about what's happened/the situation..."*
- *"It is very natural to be sad, angry, upset or..."*
- *"I hear what you are saying, about having to..."*

Explore **concerns**
Explore what the child or young person is particularly worried about and what their specific concerns are.

- *"Tell me a bit about what worries you."*
- *"Is there anything else that worries you?"*
- *"I sense that there is something more on your mind..."*

Normalise and **name reactions**

- *"In this situation, how you are feeling and how you want to react is very natural..."*

Explore **options**

- *"It can be overwhelming, so maybe we can talk about how to help you manage those difficult feelings."*
- *"Maybe we can discuss possible ways around this/solutions..."*

Key phrases you might consider using when talking about war

It can be useful to identify specific phrases you can use when initially talking to a child or young person about war and conflict. Being prepared is key as very often we can feel overwhelmed ourselves and struggle to find the appropriate language which is both affirming and calming in turn.

Things you can say might include the following:

- Lots of people feel the same way as you do. It's natural for human beings to feel so sad when other people in the world are hurting so much.

- It can be really frightening when we see fighting and wonder if it might happen in our country or town. It isn't happening anywhere near us at the moment though, but if this changes I'll be sure to tell you. We can check together whenever you feel you need to.
- It's totally understandable you feel worried about all of this. It's really hard hearing about people dying or being killed in this way.
- It's important that you asked these big questions so that you can understand what's happening around you.
- We all find it difficult to understand how people can behave in this way and hurt other human beings.

The emotion coaching process

A Trigger situation

Validation of emotions *(empathetic listening).* Help child to label their emotions, then affirm and empathise with the emotion. Allow to calm down. You look angry...and I can understand that...

Limit set separate emotion from actions

Allow more space to calm down

"That behaviour is not acceptable"

Solutions
"How do you think you will react next time?"
"Try and do this next time you feel like this."

Problem solving
Identify more appropriate and productive ways of expressing and managing feelings.
"Let's think of what we could have done instead."

Explore the feelings once calmer
Be specific.
"What did it make you feel like?"
"When did you last feel like this?"

PAGE
16

Understanding and **Supporting**
Refugee Children and **Young People:**
A Practical Resource for Teachers, Parents and
Carers of Those Exposed to the Trauma of War

The **need** for **honesty** and **age-appropriate** language

It is of course, vital that we are honest with our children and young people about what is happening. We need to answer their questions in an authentic and open way, making use of simple and clear information which is presented calmly. Taking account of the developmental age or stage of the child is also absolutely vital. We need to use language that they can understand and relate to. Clearly this will change in the light of their expressive and receptive language development.

It's also really vital that we acknowledge and recognise the level of uncertainty and unpredictability in war. We will not have all the answers and we need to give a clear message that it is okay not to know everything. It might be uncomfortable living with such a level of uncertainty but unfortunately this is the reality of the situation when we are dealing with war and conflict.

Things you **can say might include** the **following**:

- None of us can be sure when this war will end and it's tough not knowing isn't it?
- Sometimes it's hard to understand why leaders choose to start a war. I can't really understand it myself as it doesn't make sense to me either.
- Lots of people are confused about this situation and can't understand why people are fighting.
- We all wish this could end but we can't be certain when that might happen.
- We are all facing the same uncertainty but at least we can do it together and look after each other.

The **importance** of **fact checking**

We know that children and young people are often exposed to information the adults are unable to effectively monitor. This is the reality of living in the age of social media and online activity. We know that some of our older children in particular will be accessing graphic images and information via a range of different apps including tick-tock, Instagram, and Twitter for example. They may also hear news from their friends and also share images from conflict zones including live videos of experiences from YouTube or Google.

It is therefore important to find out what the child or young person is actually accessing and what they know about the whole situation. Asking them directly what information they've accessed, what pictures or videos they've seen, and what their friends are saying about the fighting for example can be a hard but necessary task. Rather than being accusatory or confrontational it is important to simply wonder with them *i.e.,* **being curious and not furious**.

Teenagers are capable of discussing some of the complexities of propaganda, fake news and misinformation that is available online and in various news channels. Many will have accessed opportunities to discuss social media via their PSHE or wellbeing curriculum and have been provided with opportunities to critically appraise imagery and content. It can be helpful to build on this when thinking about conflict and war. It might be helpful to watch some of their social media videos with them so that you can understand what they are accessing and the impact that this might have. It can also be useful to support them in the process of critically appraising the information, asking useful questions **including the following**:

- Is this source of information accurate?
- Has this image or video been verified?
- Who was responsible for sharing this information and why do you think they're doing that?
- When was this information published?
- How can we be sure that this is accurate and true?
- What additional evidence is there to show that this is factual and reliable?
- What evidence is there to show that this is not factual and reliable?

A useful source of information which is accessible to the majority of children aged seven years and above is the BBC *Newsround* website and it can be helpful to point children and young people to this in order to access reliable and verifiable information https://www.bbc.co.uk/newsround

The **importance** of **curious conversations**

When talking about war and conflict it is important to remain curious and create as many opportunities as possible for conversation. As adults we do not always need to wait for the child to tell us about their worries or concerns or fears. We can begin the interaction ourselves, providing reassurance and asking curious questions in a range of different contexts.

Very often children and young people will feel more relaxed about talking to adults if they are not in a *one-to-one* context where they are directly facing the person who is questioning them. For some children and young people, engaging in this direct way can feel slightly uncomfortable and unnatural. Think about the conversations you have when you're walking along the street, sitting on a bus together, driving in the car or walking the dog for example. It can be easier to take the opportunity to chat when you are not *face to face* but rather alongside each other as this limits any sense of the child or young person feeling placed *'on the spot'*.

It can be helpful to develop a range of curious conversation starters. You may wish to consider some in the list below, identifying those that feel most appropriate for the developmental age and stage of the young person or child that you are nurturing or working with:

- What does your body want to do when the news is on the television and the talk is all about the war?
- When are your feelings the hardest?
- When your feelings the biggest?
- Tell me about your worries right now regarding other people who are fighting in this war?
- Are you concerned about anything specific at the moment?
- How do you make sense of what's happening at the moment?
- What do you understand about what's going on at the moment?
- When are your feelings the deepest or sharpest?
- What feelings do you experience when you hear other people talking about the war? What do you think about when you see images of the war on your phone?
- What do you notice about your body when you hear about the fighting in this war?
- Sometimes our bodies hold information that our brains are not ready to cope with yet. How is your body coping with all this fighting going on?
  - When you have a thought can you identify where that thought seems to fit inside your body?
  - What goes on in your mind when you see the news every day?
  - What do you notice about other people when they hear about the war?
  - What do you think is happening in their heads? What do you think is happening to their feelings?
  - How do you think other people feel in their bodies when they see lots of horrible images?

PAGE
18

Understanding and **Supporting**
Refugee Children and **Young People:**
A Practical Resource for Teachers, Parents and
Carers of Those Exposed to the Trauma of War

Be **aware** of **unique** **lived experience** of **each child**

It is important to remember that exposure to trauma such as war and conflict in the media can re-trigger a child's own past experiences of trauma. This triggering process may include many similar emotions that they experienced previously including fear, terror, anxiety, distress, or significant loss. For some children and young people this can result in them going back in time to places where their lives were very often in danger. This can be hugely overwhelming and distressing for some who will subsequently need an approach which is entirely trauma-informed and sensitive in terms of discussing war and conflict.

As adults working with children and young people both in and out of the school context, it is consequently very important that we are aware of these children and young people and their specific experiences and current needs. We need to engage in watchful waiting to ensure that they do not become re-traumatised by exposure to war imagery and stories. We also need to ensure that they have the right kind of trauma-informed care and relevant bespoke therapeutic intervention as appropriate.

This greater level of sensitivity and intervention will need careful planning. It also needs to be based upon an awareness and understanding of trauma and how it impacts on a child's development overall.
More information on trauma and trauma-informed approaches can be found in chapter 3.

Finding the **helpers** and positive action

A key way to reduce anxiety in children and young people is to point them towards those who we regard as helpers. In every war and conflict there are always people who we can see trying to help others and it is important to remember the level of empathy and kindness that still exists even in a time of terror and conflict.

Sometimes we can do this quite simply by redirecting conversations about the conflict, death, and destruction to those who are providing support. These include the doctors, the humanitarian aid workers, the charities, emergency services, and local fundraisers etc. Children and young people can be encouraged to view images of such people engaging in their helping role and find stories of those who continue to support others despite experiencing huge levels of anxiety and trauma themselves. It can be helpful to ask children to put themselves into the helper's mind. What does it feel like to take on this role? Why is it so important? How would you feel helping others in such sad and traumatic times?

In order to move away from feelings of learned helplessness (*Peterson et al., 1995*), it can be useful to identify and articulate the things that we can all do, albeit small scale, which really could make a difference. It's vital to encourage children to

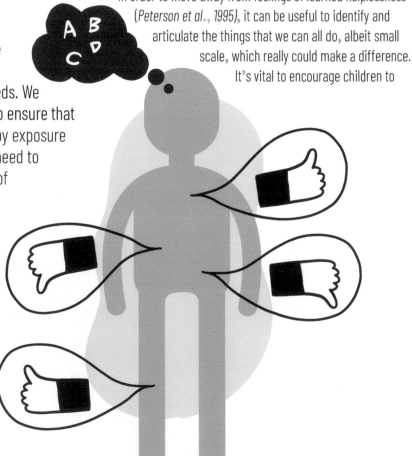

recognise the fact that we can all take on the role of the helper notwithstanding where we live, our access to financial resources or our age or culture.

Discussing with children and young people how they might take on this role can be approached individually or within the context of the school classroom. Working together to identify key tasks and making a list of these can be really useful in terms of prompting children and young people to action.

Your list might include the following:

- **Starting a petition**
- **Writing to your member of Parliament**
- **Writing poems and stories about the importance of kindness**
- **Making beautiful *'peace posters'* to share with others**
- **Writing to human rights organisations**
- **Organising fundraising events both as a family or in the school context**
- **Researching relevant charities and donating small amounts of pocket money**
- **Identifying toys, clothes, books, and other items that might be able to be donated to organisations who can distribute them to other children**
- **Engaging in rituals such as lighting candles together and wishing or praying for peace**
- **Sharing daily good news stories about those who are out there helping in the war conflict.**

5 Anxiety easy wins

It can be distressing to witness a child or young person becoming overwhelmed by a war or conflict situation but there are some very simple things that we can do in order to reduce levels of anxiety. I call these *'easy wins'* as they do not take a great deal of planning and are straightforward to implement.

1. Structure and routine

Providing structure and routine is essential. We know that when we feel in control, we have a level of certainty about what's going to happen to us in the school day for example, we would generally feel more autonomous, calm and in control. This is very important when we are living with such a level of uncertainty and being exposed to such traumatic imagery on a daily basis. Simply engaging in all the usual activities and having these planned out for and with us, can reduce the sense of hyper-arousal that many children and young people will experience.

Making use of visual timetables, to-do lists, checklists and breaking down activities into small achievable chunks can be very helpful in providing a level of structure and routine.

2. Exercise, play and free time

Ensuring that children and young people have activities scheduled in can also reduce levels of anxiety. We all know the importance of exercise for example, and the fact that it produces oxytocin, the chemical that supports us in self-regulation. It is therefore vital that children and young people have access to exercise play and free time on a daily basis.

Free time can also include elements of creativity, distraction, and grounding activities.

Providing opportunities for drawing, painting, junk modelling, clay modelling, dancing, movement and music can all help a child or young person show us how they feel, particularly if they tend not to articulate their feelings in words to any great extent.

Ensuring that the playtimes encourage socialisation and connection is also important. When we are engaged with others in fun activities it's much easier to distance our mind and hearts away from the pain towards something which is more neutral and fun. These activities can include playing word games or wordle, listening to favourite pieces of music or songs or simply cooking or baking a cake together. Watching favourite comedy shows, films and YouTube videos can also be helpful to ensure a balance of focus and distraction.

Grounding activities are particularly helpful for children and young people in order to support the removing out of the state of distress. Grounding activities help us to ground back into the here and now. **There are some simple activities you can try out and ask children to reflect upon to see which works best for them:**

1. **Going for a walk**
2. **Playing football or another ball-related game**
3. **Jumping on a trampoline**
4. **Providing a familiar or comforting smell on a piece of clothing or soft toy**
5. **Using five senses grounding identifying five things I can hear, four things I can see, three things I can touch, two things I can smell, one thing I can taste**
6. **Grounding our feet into the floor so that the soles of the feet are embedded in the floor, and we draw attention away from our busy minds to something inert**
7. **Providing additional hugs**
8. **Engaging in five finger breathing or square breathing together**
9. **Simply having some fun and laughing together**

PAGE
20

Understanding and **Supporting**
Refugee Children and **Young People:**
A Practical Resource for Teachers, Parents and
Carers of Those Exposed to the Trauma of War

Chapters 3 and *6* provide a comprehensive range of **self-regulation activities** and ideas which can be shared with children and young people and utilised by the adults who are seeking to support and nurture them.

3. **Limit access** to **news** and **social media**

Taking a digital detox can be helpful to all of us when we are attempting to reduce levels of anxiety. Much of our anxiety comes from viewing such imagery and also the resulting sense of loss of control. This needs to be modelled by adults too. We need to show children and young people that we can put our mobile phones away, focus on something creative or relaxing as opposed to being hypervigilant about what is going on in any conflict or war zone. Agreeing times when we will not access the news and information via social media and structuring these times into our day can be really helpful. It is also vital to reduce access to the news prior to bedtime. Children and young people need to go to sleep in a healthy, peaceful and anxiety reducing context. Further advice regarding sleep issues can be found in *chapter 7*.

4. **Reflect** and **focus** on **positives**

It can be difficult to remain positive when we are feeling stressed or anxious. However, simply taking time out each day to reflect on three positives can be very helpful in terms of rebalancing our experiences.

Tools from positive psychology can be very helpful here and many of these are included in *chapters 6* and *7*. Recording three good things about each day at the end of the day and planning three kind acts for the following day can take children and young people's minds away from their worries and concerns. Going to sleep at night having just focused on good things as opposed to the horror of the situation will also help support better sleep patterns. These are very simple ideas but if practised regularly and consistently they can really make a difference to a child or young person's wellbeing overall.

5. **Maintain** and **build** relationships – they **heal**

The final anxiety easy win is that of relationships. We know from the work of Bruce Perry (1994) that relationships heal. Providing young people with a sense of safety is crucial in helping them to manage and

express their distress. When they feel anxious or threatened and feel that the safety of the world is under threat, it is more important than ever to provide a sense of genuine connection to those that they trust and love.

Being that authentic, therapeutic adult who can genuinely listen and help the child process their anxieties is key to this. *Chapter 2* provides additional information on taking on this role of the therapeutic adult and the skills needed to do this effectively.

Reinforce their **sense** of **safety**

When talking about traumatic events, it is important to orient the child or young person to how they can identify and maintain a sense of safety. You can prompt them to think about this by asking a range of curious questions **including the following:**

- Who makes you feel safe in this world?
- Who makes you feel that everything is okay?
- When do you feel really safe?
- When do you feel the most relaxed?
- What positive memories can you call on about yourself, your family, or your life when you are worrying about war?

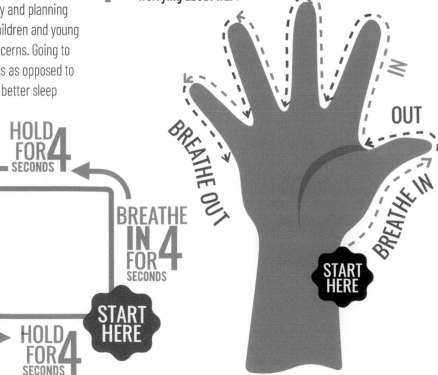

HOLD FOR 4 SECONDS
BREATHE OUT FOR 4 SECONDS
BREATHE IN FOR 4 SECONDS
HOLD FOR 4 SECONDS
START HERE

IN
OUT
BREATHE OUT
BREATHE IN
START HERE

- How can you anchor back into good times when you felt safe and relaxed when you're experiencing these worries?
- What do you do to help yourself to stay calm and chilled out?
- What can you carry in your pocket or schoolbag to help you feel settled and calm? Do you have a special photo, a lovely stone, a special piece of jewellery, or any other transitional object you could use?

Using language which focuses on keeping ourselves and others safe can also be helpful when we are dealing with such difficult and complex topics. Very often, it is simple interactions or gestures that make a difference and really help to build a greater sense of connection between the children and young people and those that they love and trust. Letting children know that we are there for them and that they're not alone can provide a sense of security. Our language needs to be both calm and reassuring. It may be helpful to consider some simple strategies **including the following**:

- **Giving additional hugs, holding hands, and cuddling up on the sofa can give a sense of safety and closeness**
- **Simply telling the child or young person that they are loved and that they are safe can also be helpful**
- **Having fun and engaging in play are probably some of the best connectors. Also, bringing a sense of playfulness and joy into each day is really essential**
- **Keeping in touch and making use of transitional objects can be helpful for younger children, or simply send additional text messages or WhatsApp messages to an older child to let them know that you are keeping them in mind while you are not physically with them**
- **For a younger child you may want to draw a heart on their hand before they leave for school so that they know when they look at it, you are thinking of them and holding them in your heart**
- **Using language of reassurance is an absolute essential. We can all say to each other** 'you are not alone, I am with you right now, I understand how you feel, your body is acting in an anxious way, but this will pass as it has done before, and you know that I am right here with you'.

Keep regulated as the supportive adult in the relationship

We know that dysregulated adults cannot possibly hope to support children in becoming regulated. They are simply not fit for purpose in terms of co-regulating and supporting others to remain within their window of tolerance. Consequently, it is vital that as adults, we all understand how we can maintain self-regulation and a sense of calm.

Developing your own tools and strategies and being able to model these for a child or young person is an essential. The next chapter in this book consequently highlights the role of the emotionally available adult and some of the techniques and strategies you can use to keep your calm and share your calm.

Chapter 4 further reinforces some of these strategies alongside highlighting how best to maintain an appropriate level of self-care in order to ensure our ability to co-regulate and maintain overall wellbeing.

CHAPTER 2
Understanding trauma in children and young people

This chapter covers

- What is trauma?
- Reinforce their sense of safety
- What is early childhood/developmental trauma?
- What the neuroscience tells us
- The unique nature of early childhood trauma
- Symptoms and behaviours
- What to look out for in both adults and children
  - *common reactions to trauma*
- A focus on the individual in school
- What we know about protecting mental health of young people after trauma - the need for resilience
- The need for a therapeutic approach – *you do not need to be a therapist*
- Taking on the role of the emotionally available adult
- Time to reflect
- Self-regulation
- Advice for the adults
- When to seek professional support for trauma
- Trauma in refugee and asylum-seeking children and young people – *an author's note*

PAGE
24

Understanding and **Supporting**
Refugee Children and **Young People:**
A Practical Resource for Teachers, Parents and
Carers of Those Exposed to the Trauma of War

What is trauma?

Trauma is used to describe both one-off events and things that are experienced over months or years, for example within a young person's family or peer relationships.

A traumatic experience often involves a threat to a young person's physical or emotional safety, and a sense of being trapped, powerless or unsupported in the face of a perceived danger or in the time afterwards.

Reinforce their sense of safety

The following are some of the traumas children and adults may experience:

- A violent or frightening event such as an assault or car accident
- Domestic violence or abuse
- Feeling unsafe at home
- Being bullied
- Losing a family member or friend to suicide, or a sudden death in the family
- Going through a physical illness or time in hospital
- Being exposed to frightening or inappropriate online content
- Living in a war zone
- Witnessing genocide.

Ultimately, whether or not an event or experience is traumatic for a young person depends on how it makes them feel as an individual. One child can find an event traumatic while another does not. The way we react to and experience what happens to us is shaped by all kinds of factors – from our personality to our life history, the support available to us, our relationships, our community, and our culture.

What is early childhood/developmental trauma?

When we are talking about early childhood trauma, we are generally making reference to the traumatic experiences that a young child may experience from the ages of 0 to 6.

It is important to remember that because children's reactions may be different in the early years compared with those of older children and young people, and they may not be able to verbalise these, many may assume that their young age protects them from these frightening and dangerous situations and experiences. However, a growing body of research has established that young children may be affected by events that threaten their safety or the safety of their parents/caregivers, and their symptoms have been well documented.

These traumas can be the result of intentional violence — such as child physical or sexual abuse, or domestic violence — or the result of natural disaster, accidents, or war. Young children also may experience traumatic stress in response to painful medical procedures or the sudden loss of a parent/caregiver.

Children 0–2 years may demonstrate:

- Poor verbal skills
- Exhibit memory problems
- Scream or cry excessively
- Have poor appetite, low weight, or digestive problems

3–6 years:

- Have difficulties focusing or learning in school
- Develop learning disabilities
- Show poor skill development
- Act out in social situations
- Imitate the abusive/traumatic event
- Be verbally abusive
- Be unable to trust others or make friends
- Believe they are to blame for the traumatic event
- Lack self-confidence
- Experience stomach aches or headaches.

We also know that when we are experiencing trauma, our thinking is hijacked by the powerful emotions this engenders. Traumatic stress as a form of toxic stress negatively impacts on learning, behaviour and relationships. It includes extremely high levels of adrenaline, cortisol and the corticotrophin releasing factor (CRF). When these levels of cortisol, and CRF are injected into animals, it results in depression, anxiety, increases in heart rate, disrupted digestion, decreased appetite, disruption of sleep, suppression of exploratory activity, startle responses, and freezing and fighting behaviour.

So, in effect, for children and young people who have experienced trauma, the more trauma they have then the more they will exhibit or experience behaviour problems and learning difficulties. Again, it's important to place this in the context of a war situation where young children will have spent a considerable amount of time having their thinking hijacked by powerful and distressing emotions.

What the neuroscience tells us

'The experience of a prolonged insecure attachment, whatever the cause, has long been suspected of producing 'invisible damage'. New methods of measurement in neuropsychology and neurobiology have been able to quantify this damage in terms of brain growth and activity. In short, we now know that parental rejection, abuse and neglect not only cause grievous developmental harm, but also grievous bodily harm.'
Cameron and **Maginn, 2008** p1152

What we now know from neuroscience is that traumatic early experiences can alter the architecture of the brain itself. Perry and Hambrick (2008) argue that the brain develops in a **neurosequential way**, starting at the brain stem which governs basic physiological survival behaviours right up to the frontal cortex which is the seat of conscious thought.

The brain will therefore develop differently, being dependent on the kind of stimulation it receives. This is provided via the physical, sensory, social and emotional environment in which a child is nurtured. The patterned rhythmic activities associated with sensitive attuned parenting produce a well-organised functional brain, but for an infant who receives chaotic or no real stimulation, the brain will present with a lack of neurological connectedness and chaotic or dysfunctional organisation.

Imaging techniques such as PET scans and MRI scans have enabled researchers to identify differences between the brains of children and adults exposed to early neglect and abuse and those brought up in a securely attached and safe context (Teicher et al., 2003).

However, more optimistically, these researchers have also been able to identify the ways in which some of this damage can be repaired as a direct result of more positive experiences of nurturing and the presence of a significantly caring adult within a safe and secure context. This is the scientific evidence to support the approach of attachment-informed care giving and trauma-informed approaches to teaching and learning.

In this approach there is therefore a focus on recognising the damage, particularly in terms of learning and emotional development, and in making the right kind of adjustments

PAGE
26

Understanding and **Supporting**
Refugee Children and **Young People:**
A Practical Resource for Teachers, Parents and
Carers of Those Exposed to the Trauma of War

and differentiating approaches to learning and behaviour management in both the home and school context.

For example, carers and teachers will need to be able to respond to children at their emotional age rather than their chronological one. Interventions and support systems for children should aim to address developmental brain impairment by providing care that can build fundamental brain capacities. For many looked-after children/traumatised children this will mean less use of verbal techniques and a greater concentration on physical, sensory and emotional ways of working and supporting them.

There will also need to be a focus on using the relationship between child and carer/teacher to address the developmental deficits and likely neurological impairments experienced by the child. This may involve focusing on touch, sensory stimulation, music and play, alongside providing a safe, predictable routine and environment for the child. This wil, in turn, ensure that the carer/teacher can support the child or young person to recognise and manage feelings and to also develop the capacity to mentalise. This will then enable them to begin to make positive relationships with others and to also begin to focus and learn within both the home and the school context.

The **unique nature** of **early childhood trauma**

When we think about a war situation in particular, it is evident that young children will have been impacted significantly in terms of their sensory needs and responses. We know that traumatic events do have a significantly profound sensory impact on younger children. Their sense of safety may be shattered by frightening visual stimuli, loud noises, violent movements, and other sensations associated with an unpredictable, frightening event.

The frightening images tend to recur in the form of nightmares, new fears, and actions or play that re-enact the event. Lacking an accurate understanding of the relationship between cause and effect, young children believe that their thoughts, wishes, and fears have the power to become real and can make things happen. Young children are less able to anticipate danger or to know how to keep themselves safe, and so are particularly vulnerable to the effects of exposure to trauma. A 2-year-old who witnesses a traumatic event like his mother being battered may interpret it quite differently from the way a 5-year-old or an 11-year-old would. Young children may blame themselves or their parents for not preventing a frightening event or for not being able to change its outcome. These misconceptions of reality compound the negative impact of traumatic effects on children's development. Young children who experience trauma are at particular risk because their rapidly developing brains are very vulnerable. Early childhood trauma has been associated with reduced size of the brain cortex. This area is responsible for many complex functions including memory, attention, perceptual awareness, thinking, language, and consciousness.

These changes may affect IQ and the ability to regulate emotions, and the child may become more fearful and may not feel as safe or as protected. Again, this supports the need for young refugee children to have their needs assessed on entry into the educational system in their new country. A regression or lack of progress may be directly linked to their experiences and some

may rebuild their skills relatively quickly; however, for those whose difficulties present as more complex there will be a need to make an appropriate cognitive assessment in order to ascertain the nature of the intervention that will be required.

Young children depend exclusively on parents/caregivers for survival and protection — both physical and emotional. When trauma also impacts the parent/caregiver, the relationship between that person and the child may be strongly affected. Without the support of a trusted parent/caregiver to help them regulate their strong emotions, children may experience overwhelming stress, with little ability to effectively communicate what they feel or need. They often develop symptoms that parents/caregivers don't understand or simply find challenging, and may display uncharacteristic behaviours that adults may not know how to appropriately respond to. For this reason, this publication also includes advice for parents, caregivers, educational professionals and specifically refugee parents as to how to effectively support their children alongside managing their own wellbeing in the process.

Symptoms and behaviours

As with older children, young children experience both behavioural and physiological symptoms associated with trauma. Unlike older children, young children cannot express in words whether they feel afraid, overwhelmed, or helpless. Young children suffering from traumatic stress symptoms generally have difficulty regulating their behaviours and emotions. They may be clingy and fearful of new situations, easily frightened, difficult to console, and/or aggressive and impulsive. They may also have difficulty sleeping, lose recently acquired developmental skills, and show regression in functioning and behaviour. Again, this is the rationale for including advice on managing these symptoms and behaviours within this publication.

What to look out for in both adults and children - common reactions to trauma

The following list of symptoms and signs can provide a useful checklist for those seeking to support children and young people in particular, as they enter into their new schools in their new refugee status. However, these common reactions are consistent across all age ranges and it is important that we are all aware of them, understand when an individual is at the top end of this continuum, and seek the appropriate support for them through specialist interventions as required.

Re-experiencing the trauma

Trauma survivors may re-experience their trauma through thoughts, feelings, memories, and other means. Re-experiencing a trauma can be very distressing, and may trigger uncomfortable emotions such as fear, anger, or sadness.

- **Nightmares**
- **Flashbacks** (*uncontrollable vivid images and memories of the trauma*)
- **Distressing thoughts and feelings about the trauma**
- **Emotional distress or physical responses after experiencing a trauma reminder.**

Avoidance of trauma reminders

Because reminders of a trauma can be so distressing, it is common for trauma survivors to use avoidance to control these reactions.

- **Using drugs or alcohol to suppress uncomfortable thoughts and emotions**
- **Avoidance of activities related to the trauma**
- **Avoidance of people, places, or things related to the trauma**
- **Suppressing thoughts related to the trauma**
- **Avoidance of conversations about the trauma**
- **Negative thoughts or feelings may begin or worsen after experiencing a trauma. Some of these thoughts and feelings might not seem to relate directly to the trauma**
- **Excessive blame toward oneself or others related to the trauma**
- **Loss of interest in activities**
- **Feelings of isolation or disconnection from surroundings**
- **Difficulty experiencing positive feelings**
- **Loss of memory related to the trauma**
- **Excessive negative thoughts about oneself or the world.**

Hyper-arousal Reactivity, or a feeling of being **"on edge"**, *may begin or worsen after experiencing a trauma.*

Understanding and Supporting
Refugee Children and Young People:
A Practical Resource for Teachers, Parents and Carers of Those Exposed to the Trauma of War

This **category includes** a **broad range** of **physical** and **psychological symptoms**.

- Becoming irritable, quick to anger, or aggressive
- Heightened startle reaction
- Difficulty concentrating
- Frequently scanning the environment or watching for trauma reminders
- Difficulty sleeping
- Feelings of anxiety, and related symptoms such as a racing heart, upset stomach, or headaches.

A focus on the individual in school

All adults in the school community not only need to be aware of trauma symptoms, but also to effectively engage in ,watchful waiting, in order to be able to quickly identify those children and young people who may be most at risk of developing more severe symptoms linked to toxic stress.

As stated previously, we now know that toxic stress due to trauma in childhood can lead to permanent changes in brain development, having significant adverse effects on memory. These findings correlate to Hanson et als., (2012) study which found that children who have experienced more intense and lasting stressful events in their lives achieved lower scores on tests of spatial working memory, and short-term memory. Lansford et al., (2002) found that students who have experienced abuse and trauma achieve poorly academically, are absent from school twice as much as their other peers and are twice as likely to be expelled from school. The long-term effects of trauma are also evident in McGloin and Widom's (2001) longitudinal study which found that only one fifth of abused and neglected children and young people experienced successful employment, only 50% completed secondary school education and over half had a psychiatric disorder.

A possible reason for these findings is that childhood trauma and its concomitant stress is likely to trap students in a physiological state of persistent alarm that makes learning in schools impossible. As Perry (2002) explains,

"When in this state, the key parts of the cortex are not receptive to cognitive information that is not relevant to survival. The traumatized child's brain is essentially unavailable to process efficiently the complex cognitive information being conveyed by the teacher...the capacity to internalize new verbal cognitive information depends upon having portions of the frontal and related cortical areas activated, which in turn requires a state of attentive calm."
(p23)

This is why many children and young people experiencing toxic stress will require mediated teaching strategies which enable them to reduce the level of working memory required and allow additional time for processing and recall. There will also be a need to focus on sensory approaches which can help to regulate the child or young person and also enable them to return to a comfort zone from which they can engage cognitively and emotionally. **Chapters 6** and **7** of this publication consequently provide a range of activities and resources to support such an objective.

What we know about protecting mental health of young people after trauma
– the need for resilience

So, we know that the effects of traumatic experiences on children and young people are sobering, but not all children are affected in the same way, nor to the same degree. Young people and their families possess competencies, psychological resources, and resilience *(often even in the face of significant trauma)* that can protect them from long-term harm.

Research on resilience in children and young people demonstrates that an essential protective factor is the reliable presence of a therapeutic, positive, caring, and protective parent or caregiver or significant other such as a teacher, who can help shield them against adverse experiences (Sroufe et al., 2005).

The need for a therapeutic approach
– you do not need to be a therapist

Although access to therapy is not seen as the **'norm'** in the majority of educational contexts, with the increase of mental health difficulties amongst our children and young people and the complex pressures that they face growing up, knowledge of therapeutic approaches is becoming essential for all who work in the educational sector. This has never been more important during times when so many children and young people are exposed to war and conflict. Also, with the dearth in specialist services and access to mental health services being significantly reduced, there is a clear imperative to provide intervention at preventative level in our schools.

The mental health leads in schools along with SENCOs and designated safeguarding leads, are taking key roles in terms of leading on whole school approaches to mental health and wellbeing.

However, at ground-level, those who are frequently asked to support children and young people with mental health difficulties both individually and in small-group contexts, are teaching assistants or learning support assistants.

*"**Schools were supporting pupils'** mental health and wellbeing in several ways. A common approach was to increase the focus on mental health in the curriculum for all pupils, often through personal, social and health education. Schools were also providing therapeutic interventions for individual pupils, often by either training their own staff or employing staff with therapeutic qualifications. Some schools were adding these roles to their pastoral teams because it has been difficult to access external services, which often had long waiting times."*

Although many staff feel relatively skilled in terms of providing academic and social support to their students, there remains a real feeling and evident concern that they do not have the knowledge base or level of skills required to specifically support those with more complex and emerging mental health difficulties.

CORPORATE REPORT
Ofsted strategy 2022–27
Published 26 April 2022

Understanding and Supporting Refugee Children and Young People:
A Practical Resource for Teachers, Parents and Carers of Those Exposed to the Trauma of War

Yet in past trials, teachers were shown to have as much, if not more positive results than psychologists as group leaders implementing the same intervention for anxious children when they were taught the same techniques and approaches as the psychologists (**Barrett** & **Turner**, 2001).

The suggestion here is not to promote the notion of staff seeking to become or take on the role of 'the therapist' but to recognise that they would be more effective in terms of identifying and preventing the escalation of such difficulties if they were more skilled and knowledgeable in utilising therapeutic skills and approaches.

Taking on the role of the emotionally available adult

When children and young people need to talk about their feelings, their emotions, their fears and anxieties, they need to do so with adults who can **truly listen,** who are non-judgemental, and who understand how to be regulated themselves so that they can share their skills and knowledge base, thus ensuring that young people can do likewise. Having a **safe space** in which to do this and knowing that the adult you are talking to will truly listen is key here for young people who may be distressed and anxious.

Research shows that the best way to alleviate anxiety as opposed to just trying to '**manage anxiety**' is to address the

feelings experienced at the time of the painful life event. That said, it is never possible to do this alone, only in the presence of an **emotionally available adult,** one who can listen and empathise and help the child/teenager to make sense of the traumatic event.

This is because the feelings about it are often deemed by the child/teenager as too dangerous to feel on their own (e.g., fear of the strength of their grief, fear of shame, fear of going mad, fear of the strength of their rage) which is why anxiety developed in the first place. As Freud said, "**anxiety protects us from fear.**"

Young children and teenagers need to know how unaddressed trauma can fuel anxiety because most of them have no idea. Anxious teenagers, for example, are often extremely aware and super eloquent about their symptoms: panic attacks, psychosomatic symptoms (after endless 'all clears' from doctors) , phobias, obsessions, heart palpitations – but not about the cause of those symptoms.

However, with supportive curious enquiry from an adult trained to listen, many will accurately and easily recall the life events that changed everything for them and left them feeling fundamentally unsafe and insecure in the world.

As Margot Sunderland states, underlying any anxiety is an impaired ability to meaningfully think about feelings. In other words, anxiety is fuelled by wordless sensations, known by some as '**unstoried emotions**'. With help from the trained

adult to make sense of the original 'trauma' the anxious child can find relief by putting painful feelings into words. As observed by Heather Geddes *(2006)*, these **'unbearable feelings'** can **transform into 'thinkable thoughts'**, meaning that a traumatic memory can evolve from a haunting nightmare into an integrated part of our life story.

Time to reflect

It is very important for adults who are seeking to take on the role of the emotionally available adult, to take some time to reflect upon their own experiences and the ways in which they have worked through their own traumas and been able to recover and learn from their experiences. It can be useful to make use of a timeline, mind map, or life map to reflect upon your own experiences as a child and an adult and how you have managed to navigate your way through more difficult situations in your life.

Think about your own levels of resilience in your own ability to bounce back when things become difficult for very tough. Also think about what strategies you currently use in order to maintain your own wellbeing. What do you do? How do you engage in self-care? How do you ensure that you can be reflective whilst also challenging your own patterns of negative automatic thinking? How can you feel confident that you will be able to maintain your wellbeing while supporting children and young people with difficulties of this nature and not become at risk of experiencing or developing vicarious trauma? Also think about what kinds of skills you may need to develop further and how making use of this publication might help you to do exactly that

A good place to start is with a focus on self-regulation.

Self-regulation

In my view, key to any intervention of this nature is the teaching and modelling of self-regulation skills. Self-regulation is the ability to understand and control your behaviour and your emotional reactions. This includes being able to calm yourself down when experiencing big emotions such as anxiety, anger, or excitement. Self-regulation skills also enable us to focus on the task at hand, and respond with socially appropriate behaviour, rather than showing how we might really feel. Self-regulation skills are important because they help children to control their impulses, maintain relationships with other children during play, and manage their stress levels. Through this self-

regulation, they are able to feel safe, content, and able to learn.

Self-regulation skills start to develop in early childhood. When children have experienced co-regulation through consistent, sensitive, and nurturing relationships, they begin to learn how to manage their own emotions. Neuroscientific research suggests that these relationships help to develop the links between the emotional limbic brain, and the cerebral cortex, allowing children to be better able to rationalise, reason, empathise and problem-solve. However, the cerebral cortex is not thought to be fully developed until the mid-twenties, and therefore children, adolescents and even us adults need support with self-regulation at times.

In adolescence, the brain is undergoing significant changes ready for adulthood, meaning that it can be more difficult for teenagers to rationalise and regulate their emotions. So, if you have ever experienced a teenager being irrational and unreasonable — it is actually not entirely their fault! This, together with an increase in dopamine, a neurochemical linked to risk-taking and impulsivity, and hormones coming into play, can be an overwhelming combination.

So, in the light of this brain development, it is vital to support teenagers to regulate their emotions **before** trying to reason with them.

PAGE
32

Understanding and Supporting
Refugee Children and Young People:
A Practical Resource for Teachers, Parents and Carers of Those Exposed to the Trauma of War

Some calming techniques to model to them and to teach them to self-regulate include:

- Mindfulness
- Visualisation
- Grounding
- Sensory activities
- Controlled breathing.

These techniques have been incorporated into **chapter 6** of this resource, along with activities designed to help children and young people identify and process their emotions. Research shows us that labelling emotions can help to reduce the intensity of the emotion (*Torre & Lieberman, 2018*), and therefore teaching this skill is integral in helping them to manage their own emotions.

Advice for the adults

It is important that all adults seeking to support children and young people as they recover from trauma are themselves nurtured and protected and have access to an appropriate level of support. For some, this may mean a more intensive specialist therapeutic intervention. For many, this can simply mean engaging in a series of trauma recovery activities, all of which have been found to work and have a clear evidence base.

Whether or not a traumatic event involves death, the survivor must cope with the loss, at least temporarily, of their sense of safety. The natural reaction to this loss is grief. Like people who have lost a loved one, we will need to go through a grieving process. The following tips can help us to cope with the sense of grief, heal from the trauma, and move on with our lives:

Trauma recovery
Tip 1: Get moving

Trauma disrupts your body's natural equilibrium, freezing you in a state of hyper-arousal and fear. As well as burning off adrenaline and releasing endorphins, exercise and movement can help to repair your nervous system.

Try to exercise for 30 minutes or more on most days. Or if it is easier, three 10-minute spurts of exercise per day are just as good.

Exercise that is rhythmic and engages both your arms and legs — such as walking, running, swimming, or even dancing — works best.

Add a mindfulness element. Instead of focusing on your thoughts or distracting yourself while you exercise, really focus on your body and how it feels as you move. Notice the sensation of your feet hitting the ground, for example, or the rhythm of your breathing, or the feeling of wind on your skin. Rock climbing, boxing, weight training, or martial arts can make this easier as you need to focus on your body movements during these activities in order to avoid injury.

Tip 2: Don't isolate

Following a trauma, you may want to withdraw from others, but isolation only makes things worse. Connecting to others face to face will help you heal, so make an effort to maintain your relationships and avoid spending too much time alone.

You don't have to talk about the trauma. Connecting with others doesn't have to involve talking about the trauma. In fact, for some people, that can just make things worse. Comfort comes from feeling engaged and accepted by others and, as Bruce Perry (*2002*) says '*relationships heal*'.

Ask for support. While you don't have to talk about the trauma itself, it is important that you have someone to share your feelings with face to face, someone who will listen attentively without judging you. Turn to a trusted family member, friend, or counsellor who specialises in trauma recovery.

Participate in social activities, even if you don't feel like it. Do "*normal*" activities with other people, activities that have nothing to do with the traumatic experience.

Reconnect with old friends. If you've retreated from relationships that were once important to you, make the effort to reconnect.

Join a support group for trauma survivors/survivors of war. Connecting with others who are facing the same problems can help reduce your sense of isolation, and hearing how others cope can help inspire you in your own recovery.

Volunteer. As well as helping others, volunteering can be a great way to challenge the sense of helplessness that often accompanies trauma. Remind yourself of your strengths and reclaim your sense of power by helping others.

Make new friends. If you live alone or far from family and friends, it's important to reach out and make new friends to avoid compounding any sense of isolation. Find organisations where you can meet up with others, learn new things or simply connect with other like-minded people who understand the need to connect and support each other.

Tip **3**: Self-regulate your nervous system

No matter how agitated, anxious, or out of control you feel, it's important to know that you can change your arousal system and calm yourself. Not only will it help relieve the anxiety associated with trauma, but it will also engender a greater sense of control.

Mindful breathing. If you are feeling disoriented, confused, or upset, practising mindful breathing is a quick way to calm yourself. Simply take 60 breaths, focusing your attention on each '*out*' breath.

Sensory input. Does a specific sight, smell or taste quickly make you feel calm? Or maybe petting an animal or listening to music works to quickly soothe you? Everyone responds to sensory input a little differently, so experiment with different quick stress relief techniques to find what works best for you.

Staying grounded. To feel in the present and more grounded, sit on a chair. Feel your feet on the ground and your back against the chair. Look around you and pick six objects that have red or blue in them. Notice how your breathing gets deeper and calmer.

Allow yourself to feel what you feel when you feel it. Acknowledge your feelings about the trauma as they arise and accept them.

Tip **4**: Take care of your health

It is a given that having a healthy body can and does increase our ability to cope with the stress of trauma. This is an essential and basic common-sense.

Get plenty of sleep. After a traumatic experience, worry or fear may disturb your sleep patterns. But a lack of quality sleep can exacerbate your trauma symptoms and make it harder to maintain your emotional balance. Go to sleep and get up at the same time each day and aim for 7 to 9 hours of sleep each night.

Avoid alcohol and drugs. Their use can worsen your trauma symptoms and increase feelings of depression, anxiety, and isolation.

Eat a well-balanced diet. Eating small, well-balanced meals throughout the day will help you keep your energy up and minimise mood swings. Avoid sugary and fried foods and eat plenty of omega-3 fats to give your mood a boost.

Reduce stress. Try relaxation techniques such as meditation, yoga, or deep breathing exercises. Schedule time for activities that bring you joy such as your favourite hobbies or creative activities. Again, this publication provides you with a range of different tools and strategies to reduce stress and create your own self care plan.

When to seek professional support for trauma

We know that recovering from trauma takes time. We also know that every individual is different and will heal at their own pace. However, both children and adults alike may need additional support from a specialist trauma therapist or counsellor should the symptoms of trauma remain significant after many months have passed. This is the rationale for maintaining a vigilant regime in terms of observing symptoms in both the home and school context and keeping a record to identify whether or not symptoms are reducing over time.

Children and adults should seek help for their trauma if they are:

- **Having trouble functioning at home, school or work**
- **Suffering from severe fear, anxiety, or depression**
- **Unable to form close, satisfying relationships**
- **Experiencing terrifying memories, nightmares, or flashbacks**
- **Avoiding more and more anything that reminds them of the trauma**
- **Emotionally numb and disconnected from others**
- **Using alcohol or drugs to feel better.**

Research regarding evidence-based practice in this area details how working through trauma can be scary, painful, and potentially re-traumatising, so this healing work is best undertaken with the help of an experienced trauma specialist.

PAGE
34

Understanding and **Supporting**
Refugee Children and **Young People:**
A Practical Resource for Teachers, Parents and
Carers of Those Exposed to the Trauma of War

Trauma in refugee and asylum-seeking children and young people

– an **author's** note

This chapter has attempted to provide an overview of trauma, early childhood trauma and some simple ways in which we can all begin to engage in post-trauma growth. I have also highlighted the need for us all to engage with our children and young people, specifically our refugees, in a more therapeutic and nurturing way in order to help them to feel safe and recognise that they can and will heal over time.

In my own role as an educational and child psychologist I have worked with many unaccompanied children and young people seeking asylum. I have encountered children and young people who have been exposed to political discord, violence, death, torture, and so much more as an outcome of war. In the course of this work, I have seen how devastating, complex and wide-ranging the impact of war can be on children's lives.

So many of these children and young people have been separated from their parents because of war. Many have witnessed or experienced violence, torture, abuse and death. Some have been severely injured, or been left with lifelong physical disabilities and discomfort, or developed preventable diseases. Some children are also recruited as soldiers themselves. Many are subjected to sexual violence, trafficking, grooming and child pregnancy.

War has an enormous impact on childhood in other ways. Destruction of the local economy, agriculture and infrastructure can lead to children needing to work in order to eat, children having to be caregivers to younger siblings, or ending up on the streets due to extreme poverty. They might be forced to move into refugee or displaced person camps, short or long term. Education is disrupted, or there is none at all.

We know that the psychological effects of war and war-related trauma can be severe. Some children may experience PTSD associated with specific events. Others may have more complex developmental trauma from long-term exposure to extreme adversity. Children struggle to understand the causes of the conflict – their exposure is to the chaos and disruption.

This can lead to depression, severe anxiety, and associated dysregulation in daily functioning such as sleep, appetite, focus, concentration and memory. Children might seem lethargic or agitated, experience ruminations, negative self-beliefs or lack of pleasure, and engage in substance use, self-harm and suicide attempts.

This can leave us, as adults, feeling helpless in the face of such despair and terror. However, for many professionals in the school context there will not be an expectation that they should take on the role of a specialist trauma intervention worker or psychologist.

What we can all do, however, is to develop our own skills and knowledge so that we can effectively provide refugee children with a safe space, opportunities for self-regulation and support to process some of their losses in a nurturing relationship. This is something that we can all undertake and consequently the focus of the next chapter in this publication which aims to empower you to support refugee children and young people more effectively as they enter the school context.

CHAPTER 3
Supporting refugee children and young people

This chapter covers

- What is it that actually works in terms of supporting our refugee children in the school and social context?
- Refugee support plan
- 6 main areas of support
- The importance of whole school approaches to educating about refugees
- What they all need to know
- Assessing the need for additional support and what we can all do at the start
- 6 keys to a trauma-informed classroom
- The power of safe spaces to promote self-regulation
- Creating safe spaces for all
- The Window of Tolerance
- What we can do
- 5 Keys to setting up the safe space
- Key tools and strategies
- Moving from hyper-arousal to the *Window* of *Tolerance*
- Moving from hypo-arousal to the *Window* of *Tolerance*
- Additional wellbeing support tools
- Expressive writing approaches
- Tree of life
- Physical activities
- Loss and bereavement support
- What might you observe if a child is experiencing grief?
- Cultural factors
- Referring on
- An important point

PAGE
38

Understanding and **Supporting**
Refugee Children and **Young People:**
A Practical Resource for Teachers, Parents and
Carers of Those Exposed to the Trauma of War

Supporting refugee Children and Young People

We know that trauma in refugee children will be a significant factor to consider when beginning to develop programmes of support and interventions to integrate them into the school community. Refugees and asylum-seeking children and young people have a more elevated risk for psychological difficulties than other '***newcomers***' *(Kim et al., 2018).* They are less likely to be prepared for migration and more likely to have limited or interrupted education prior to arriving in the host country *(Taylor & Sidhu, 2012).*

Research focusing on war-affected children and young people has shown very strong correlation between the number of traumatic events they have experienced and the intensity of these with the likelihood of them developing significant psychological distress *(McMullen et al., 2012).* This has been backed up by other research studies which show how cumulative exposure to traumatic events is directly linked to subsequent psychological problems and difficulties *(Derluyn & Broekaert, 2007).*

It's also important to note that when a child has encountered more severe types of trauma such as the violent death of a family member or witnessing someone close to them being killed, they will naturally experience heightened levels of distress as a result *(McMullen et al., 2012; Reed et al., 2012).*

A systematic review which looked at the mental health of refugee children who had effectively resettled into higher income countries, found that their exposure to violence in their home country was perceived to be a significant risk factor for subsequent healthy psychological development. An effective integration which provides a heightened level of safety and security alongside the development

Creating a clear idea of the way foreward with a Refugee Support Plan

of social support in both the school and social contexts were both found to have a significantly positive effect on the individuals' psychological functioning *(Reed et al., 2012).*

What is absolutely vital is to have a clear understanding of the specific needs of individual refugee children. Much of the research shows us that they are clearly not 'all the same' in their psychological presentation, so identifying needs at the outset is vital. This needs to be supported by a phased model of intervention with appropriate support systems in place *(Ehntholt & Yule, 2006; Kim et al., 2018).*

A key point to note, which is reinforced in my **Refugee Support Plan**, is that not all refugee children and young people will present with post-traumatic stress disorder or significant levels of anxiety as a result of what they have experienced in the nature of each young person's experience and specific strengths within their communities. Many of them will display resilience, resourcefulness, and relatively high levels of functioning despite the difficulties and trauma that they may have experienced. *(Ehntholt & Yule 2006; McMullen et al., 2012).*

So, in line with the British Psychological Society's guidelines for psychologists working with refugees and asylum seekers in the UK, I would suggest that it is vitally important that we do not pathologise the suffering of refugee families and their children.

For many children and young people, the way in which they present will simply be a normal response to extremely abnormal experiences. We therefore need to take a holistic perspective and recognise the diverse nature of each young person's experiences
(BPS, 2018; Rutter, 2006).

We therefore need to take a holistic perspective and recognise the diverse nature of each young person's experiences, the levels of experience and specific strengths within their communities *(BPS, 2018; Rutter, 2006).* If we treat refugees as a homogeneous group, this risks individuals, masking their experiences. This can be problematic because those attempting to support them in the school-based contexts may be unable to accurately identify their real needs and subsequent interventions that need to be put in place in order to support them *(Rutter, 2006).*

However, what is apparent from all the relevant research is the fact that, regardless of the child or young person's traumatic experiences, access to the school context as quickly as possible on entry to the country, is the most effective means of supporting integration into the new community and subsequently ensuring an improvement in their quality of life *(BPS, 2018).*

We now know that there is a growing body of evidence which suggests that schools are probably the most appropriate place to identify, address and meet the needs of our refugee children and young people. Within the school context they are able to build their levels of resilience and also increase their capacity for learning *(Fazel, 2015).* In essence, the level of stability, routine, and security that school can provide on a daily basis will be the key factor in providing structure to their daily lives and enhancing overall wellbeing *(McMullen et al., 2020; Rutter, 2006).*

In other words, **school really is the best medicine**. It is important to hold onto this fact when attempting to integrate and support refugee children to engage in post-trauma growth and successfully find their place in their new social and educational contexts.

What is it that **actually works** in terms of **supporting** our **refugee children** in the **school** and **social context**?

I have developed a refugee support plan which encapsulates many of the key points from this chapter, including reference to the research which supports the advice provided. This can be helpful to share with school-based staff, parents, and carers in order to clarify what works in practice and also demystify these approaches.

It is vital to understand that there is so much we can do in the school context to effectively support and nurture our refugee children as they come into our schools, and to flag up the fact that much of this is essentially good practice in terms of supporting all our children who may exhibit elements of stress, anxiety, and trauma-related behaviours.

It can be helpful to share this and use it as a tool for discussion amongst the staff group or parent groups.

Understanding and Supporting
Refugee Children and Young People:
A Practical Resource for Teachers, Parents and
Carers of Those Exposed to the Trauma of War

Refuge
support
plan

Refugee children may well be experiencing **fear, terror, and helplessness** as they transition into our schools and communities

Empathy is key as is the need to become a **school of sanctuary** where they feel **safe** and **included**

Flexibility is crucial as all **refugee children are different** - some will want and need to talk straight away, others will not, and may need time to process their experiences or do so in more creative ways through play, art, and creative outlets

Understanding the *symptoms of trauma* and what to look for is also key - avoidance, re-enactment, withdrawal, or aggression

Get down to their level, **hear the voice of the child** - '*this is what I do want*' '*This is what I don't want or need right now*' – not every child needs a bespoke therapeutic intervention so keep using your *watchful* waiting skills

Express a *genuine welcome* as their *new nurturer* – '*we want you here in our school community, we value you and will make sure that you are safe and loved*'

Engage with *parents and carers in the community* remembering that **practical help and advice is often a helpful starting point**

Set up welcoming *signs and systems* such as labelling/visual timetables etc. in their own language and involve parents and carers to translate

Understanding that they need *respite from anxiety* - a face may light up if you ask about their favourite football team rather than their journey to the UK

Provide an *accessible curriculum* and climate of welcome which uses the skills and empathy of their peer group

Promote *play, socialisation and physical activity and opportunities for flow* experiences

Observe their **existing skill set** and show you value this - tell me about what you know, what you are interested in and what you are good at, *always allowing for a regression due to trauma*

Respect their need to simply '*fit in*' and '*be normal*', nurturing resilience through *love, empowerment, engagement, connection, and the development of coping skills*

The **key is school itself** - simply '*being in school*' is the best medicine for our refugee children - providing safety, security and routine which will enable their post-traumatic growth and give them the hope so needed by all right now.

PAGE
42

Understanding and **Supporting**
Refugee Children and **Young People:**
A Practical Resource for Teachers, Parents and
Carers of Those Exposed to the Trauma of War

6 MAIN AREAS OF SUPPORT

1. Ask for help and support

- Seek support from existing agencies including the psychological service and those currently working with refugees

- Share best practice knowing that there are many out there who have developed effective ways of working with these children and young people

- Ask refugee parents to assist in translation of key terminology

- Ensure adequate training in the effects of trauma so that all staff are empowered to develop trauma-informed approaches

- Ask local charities to support with provision of materials including PE kits, writing tools *etc.*

2. Provide induction
Refugee children will benefit if teachers and schools:

- Respect their right to a silent period *(sometimes lasting several months)* **or to not talk about recent events**

- Give them opportunities to talk, sensitively and not initially in front of an audience of other children, about their family history and their recent circumstances if they feel this is appropriate and they are comfortable in doing so – but be very vigilant about this as many may simply want and need to simply *'fit in'* and not remember/recall certain events for some time

- Find out about any religious or dietary requirements they may have

- Ensure that their names are pronounced and spelt properly by all staff

- ensure they know the names of other pupils and other adults that they will meet, *(particularly lunchtime supervisors and break time staff)*

- Teach *'survival'* school and classroom terminology including toilet, book, desk, playtime, *etc.*, and other important words

- Display key vocabulary for particular subjects in both English and, where possible, the child's first language

- Familiarise children with the layout of the school, playground, rules, expectations, and routines

- Check on their wellbeing after break times

- Arrange for relevant local authority specialist staff to make visits home to involve parents or guardians of refugee children to as great an extent as possible

- Emphasise to parents or carers the importance of maintaining the children's first language.

3. Utilise the skills of other children

- Arrange for introductions to any other same-language pupils and families

- Establish a *'buddy'* system which has status, is supervised, and monitored, involves a range of children, not just the usual helpful pupils, and is the focus of classroom work and discussion

- Encourage older, or more familiar, refugee children to provide support and comfort to newcomers

- Involve other pupils in making a book, or photographic record, or perhaps a film about the school that children can take home to show their families

- Ensure they have *'tools'* for homework such as pencils, colours, and other necessary items.

4. Create a *'climate'* in which refugee children feel welcome and valued
Schools can do this by:

- Being sensitive to religious observances and dietary needs
- Structuring discussions about refugees, empathy, diversity, mutual respect, and human rights within relevant places in the curriculum
- Approaching refugee children as resources for learning
- Encouraging use of home languages where appropriate, *e.g.*, all pupils could learn greetings and goodbyes
- Using multilingual signs around the school and displays of representative cultural items
- Obtaining or involving pupils in creating multilingual dictionaries, storybooks and other resources
- Identifying and giving praise to children's strengths and successes
- Using correct and precise language in clear *'easy to hear'* sentences.

5. Make the curriculum accessible
This includes:

- Making purposes and goals as clear as possible
- Using drama, puppets, art, mime, and pictorially based tasks – including photographs, charts, flow diagrams, storyboards, maps
- Ensuring that achievements in subjects which are less language-based, *e.g.*, mathematics, science, and PE, are recognised
- Assessing literacy and English language skills
- Using bilingual dictionaries and web-based translators and apps
- Maximising use of ICT
- Using cards, draughts, chess, backgammon, dominoes, noughts and crosses and board games, which may already be familiar, perhaps in different forms, as learning resources and to encourage interaction with peers
- Playing music and singing songs
- Using pictures for labelling, matching, sorting, classifying
- Using books with a strong visual content, or no words, for a range of year groups
- Making available a wide variety of mathematical apparatus
- Providing audio visual support; taped stories and other ICT based support tools.

6. Classroom organisation

- Grouping refugee children with other children and young people as language models
- Encouraging all pupils to bring in toys, artefacts, and/or photographs so they can share *stories*, interests and hobbies
- Generating discussion about pupils' common experiences of change, moving home, being frightened and loss
- Exploring with pupils visual, non-verbal methods of communication, *e.g.*, body language, facial expressions
- Prioritising interactive activities which encourage collaboration between pupils and help to speed up English language acquisition, for example, information gap activities and barrier games
- Emphasising listening and speaking skills
- Using dolls, artefacts, toys, food, and other *'everyday'* items as teaching aids; and using tickets, shopping lists, bills, *'everyday'* documents, newspapers, and magazines.

PAGE
44

Understanding and Supporting
Refugee Children and Young People:
A Practical Resource for Teachers, Parents and Carers of Those Exposed to the Trauma of War

The importance of whole school approaches to educating about refugees

One key element of the support system that we can create is that of introducing the whole concept of refugees, highlighting specific definitions, ensuring understanding among staff and children and young people, and tackling, at the outset, any element of stigma or potential bullying that may arise when refugee children enter the school context.

A refugee is a person outside his or her country who is unable or unwilling to return to receive protection from that country because of persecution or a well-founded fear of persecution due to race, religion, nationality, membership in a particular social group, or political opinion.

We need to initially create awareness among students, teachers, school support and office staff, school management and governors about:

- Why people become refugees
- Where refugees come from
- The difference between refugees and asylum seekers and other migrants
- Why refugees come to the UK and to your city
- Why some refugees are destitute
- Why refugees and asylum seekers need protection.

What they all need to know

A survey by the Refugee Council in 2011 (https://issuu.com/refugeecouncil/docs/refugee_council_impact_report_2011_12/23) found that **82%** of British people believe protecting the most vulnerable is a core British value. However, negative attitudes towards asylum seekers, fuelled by incorrect media headlines, are common. Many people get confused between asylum seekers and economic migrants and think asylum seekers are here to get jobs or benefits. In fact, an asylum seeker is someone who says their life is in danger in their own country and has applied to stay in the UK. The UK asylum system is extremely tough.

People often get moved around whilst their claim is decided and there is a lot of uncertainty. Housing is often substandard and financial support is low. Refugees make a huge contribution to the UK. 18 refugees have become Nobel Laureates, 16 refugees have received knighthoods. Many refugees are doctors, nurses, or teachers.

Seeking out useful resources and stories for children and young people which aim to tackle stigma and ensure a genuine understanding of the experiences of refugee children and their families can be very useful. *The following Publications may be helpful to achieve such an objective:*

The Colour of Home by *Mary Hoffman*

The story of Hassan's first day at an English school, after his family flee war in Somalia. It describes his sadness and how the school helps him feel welcome and settled. **For ages 5-11.**

The Librarian of Basra by *Jeanette Winter*

The true story of a librarian's struggle to save her community's collection of books during the war in Iraq. **For ages 5-11.**

The Silence Seeker by *Ben Morley*

When a new family moves next door, Joe's mum explains that they are asylum seekers. Joe hears that they are silence seekers, especially as Mum adds that they need peace and quiet. When he sees a young boy from the family sitting disconsolately on the steps, Joe decides to help him find a quiet place in the noisy and chaotic city. **For ages 5-7.**

Refugee Boy by *Benjamin Zephaniah*

The story of Alem, a young boy forced to live in London whilst his parents face separation from their son and from each other at the time of the Ethiopian-Eritrean war. **For ages 11+.** Session plans available:
http://www.britishcouncil.org/refugee_boy_session_1.pdf
(10 sessions available)

The Other Side of Truth by *Beverley Naidoo*.

Two shots at the gate in the early morning and a car screeches away down an avenue of palm trees. A tragedy—and a terrible loss for Sade and her younger brother Femi, children of an outspoken Nigerian journalist. Now terror is all around them and they must flee their country. Plans for their journey have to be hastily arranged. Everything must be done in secret. But once Sade and Femi reach England, they will be safe—won't they?
For ages 12+.

Assessing the need for additional support and what we can all do at the start

Alongside ensuring that the six main areas of support are addressed in terms of integrating our refugee children, it will be necessary to engage in '*watchful waiting*' in terms of identifying those children and young people who may, potentially, require additional specialist therapeutic input in the longer term.

However, it is vital to allow time for the child or young person to express their needs either verbally or through their behaviours. Consequently, understanding how trauma is held in the body and may not display itself for many months or years is clearly an essential, as is the need to hear the voice of the child and actually engage in identifying what is really going to meet their needs at any given time. Keeping the door open in terms of providing access to additional support is an essential. It is therefore important that all refugee children are made aware of what support is available to them in the school context.

This may involve a range of therapeutic interventions delivered by the school's mental health lead, educational and child psychologist, or other external agencies. For some this will involve narrative therapy approaches, access to cognitive behaviour therapy (*CBT*) approaches or other specialist therapeutic input.

At the outset, it is important to flag up the fact that many schools will have a range of interventions in place which can effectively meet the needs of refugee children and young people in the first instance.

Developing an awareness of trauma-informed approaches and creating trauma-informed classrooms will be key here.

As stated in the introduction, the trauma-informed classroom ensures that all children can feel safe, nurtured, and included.

There are six key areas we can focus on right now:

6 keys to a trauma-informed classroom:

1. Belonging	- making sure the children feel welcomed, wanted and part of the group
2. Predictability	- making sure that changes to routines are explained clearly and with empathy
3. Organisation	- ensuring that the routines and activities are consistent and visual checklists are provided as necessary
4. Regulation	- teaching an emotional literacy curriculum and ensuring a safe space of calm corner is available to children and young people and that they understand how to use this effectively in order to self-regulate
5. Differentiation	- reduce processing demands in the classroom and provide clear structures or plans for each task
6. Relationships	- keep connections healthy and empathic, modelling social skills and valuing and celebrating their strengths and achievements.

PAGE
46

Understanding and **Supporting**
Refugee Children and **Young People:**
A Practical Resource for Teachers, Parents and
Carers of Those Exposed to the Trauma of War

The **power** of **safe spaces** to **promote self-regulation**

We know that regulation is a key area of development for all our children and young people and adults alike. However, for our refugee children and young people coming into school, it is really vital that we provide them with calm corners or safe spaces where they can retreat *(with support if necessary)* in order to engage in self-regulation activities and take time out when they feel overwhelmed by their new surroundings and the level of the demands that this may make both socially and cognitively.

Teaching key tools and strategies from a range of therapeutic approaches will benefit all young people and can be seen as part of a whole school approach to developing and maintaining wellbeing.

Again, it is important to note that you do not need to be a therapist or have any specific therapeutic training to deliver this kind of intervention.

Creating **safe spaces** for **all**

Creating your safe spaces in which children and young people can learn how to regulate and develop tools and strategies so that they can remain in their window of tolerance is an essential task. The safe space or sanctuary needs to be a special place of safety where children and young people can give themselves greater opportunities to be resilient and stay calm and focused. Developing their self-awareness and with this, greater levels of adaptability, flexibility and independence are the key objectives of such a space.

The **Window** of **Tolerance**

The Window of Tolerance is a model founded in neuroscience and helps develop good practice for improving and maintaining mental health and wellbeing. It presents us with information as to how we function at our best, in all areas of our lives so that we can manage when emotions become difficult, complex, or seemingly overwhelming.

We know that children's emotions fluctuate, particularly at times of stress and crisis and they can find it hard to put their feelings into words. We need therefore to be able to recognise this sense of overwhelm and to know when and why they are struggling with their feelings and emotions. Using the Window of Tolerance provides us with a way to do this.

HOW TRAUMA CAN AFFECT YOUR WINDOW OF TOLERANCE

Each person's window of tolerance is different. Those who have a narrow window of tolerance may often feel as if their emotions are intense and difficult to manage. Others with a wider window of tolerance may be able to handle intense emotions or situations without feeling like their ability to function has been significantly impacted.

When a person is within their window of tolerance, it is generally the case that the brain is functioning well and can effectively process stimuli. That person is likely to be able to reflect, think rationally, and make decisions calmly without feeling either overwhelmed or withdrawn.

During times of extreme stress, people often experience periods of either hyper- or hypo-arousal. It is important that we distinguish between the two, and particularly in terms of supporting our refugee children and young people. Many will experience both forms of arousal at some point as they integrate into the school context.

How **trauma** can affect your **window of tolerance**

When stress and trauma shrink your window of tolerance, it doesn't take much to throw you off balance.

Hyper

Hypo

Hyper-arousal
Anxious, Angry, Out of Control, Overwhelmed
Your body wants to fight or run away.
It's not something you choose - these reactions just take over.

Window of Tolerance
When you are in your Window of Tolerance you feel like you can deal with whatever's happening in your life. You might feel stress or pressure but it doesn't bother you too much.
This is the ideal place to be.

Hypo-arousal
Spacy, Zoned Out, Frozen
Your body wants to shut down.
It's not something you choose – these reactions just take over.

Working with a practitioner can help expand your window of tolerance so that you are more able to cope with challenges.

Hyper

Hypo

What **we can do**

It is possible for individuals who have become dysregulated to use techniques to return to their window of tolerance. Grounding and Mindfulness skills, techniques considered beneficial by many mental health experts, can often help people remain in the present moment. By focusing on the physical sensations currently being experienced, for example, people are often able to remain in the present, calming and soothing themselves enough to effectively manage extreme arousal.

Many children and adults are able to widen their window of tolerance and, by doing so, increase their sense of calm and become able to deal with stress in more adaptive ways. We know that therapeutic relationships and trauma-informed contexts and spaces can provide a safe space for people to process painful memories and emotions, and make contact with their emotions without becoming so dysregulated that they cannot integrate them. Increasing emotional regulation capabilities in this way can lead to a wider window of tolerance and prevent dysregulation.

During times of extreme stress, people often experience periods of either **hyper-** or **hypo-arousal**. It is important that we distinguish between the two, and particularly in terms of supporting our refugee children and young people. Many will experience both forms of arousal at some point as they integrate into the school context.

Hyper-arousal, otherwise known as the **flight/fight** response, is often characterised by **hypervigilance**, feelings of **anxiety and/or panic**, and **racing thoughts**.

Hypo-arousal, or a **freeze response**, may cause feelings of **emotional numbness**, **emptiness**, or **paralysis**.

In either of these states, an individual may become unable to process stimuli effectively. The prefrontal cortex region of the brain shuts down, in a manner of speaking, **affecting the ability to think rationally and often leading to the development of feelings of dysregulation**, which may take the form of **chaotic responses** or **overly rigid ones**. In these periods, a person can be said to be outside the window of tolerance.

5 Keys to setting up the safe space
Key 1 Location

It is important to carefully consider where you will set up your safe space. For example, you may choose a space in the back of the room, so students using it do not feel self-conscious. The best option of course is to have a dedicated room, but this is a luxury for many in today's current climate. **Ask yourself**:

- **Does the space have enough room for a chair/small sofa/bean bag and possibly a small table?**
- **Does the space seem semi-private?**
- **Can children easily access the space?**

Key 2 Furniture

Furniture is another key factor in creating your safe space. The size of the space will determine what you can include. At a minimum, you will need an adequate seating area which includes a chair/bean bag/small sofa. A small desk or table will also be useful for any self-reflection/recording activities as will a listening booth for access to music tapes/relaxation tapes/online calm down resources.

Key 3 Meaningful visuals

You will need to provide children with visual displays and resources to help them self-regulate and manage their emotions.
For example:

- **A poster with breathing techniques**
- **A poster asking students to rate their "*emotional temperature*"**
- **A list of things they could do in the Safe space**
- **A resource with strategies for problems solving in a stepped way**
- **A resource with strategies for using key tools from Mindfulness such as visualisation of my place/grounding of my feet to the floor.**

Key 4 Calm down tools

A calm face space is not complete without the physical/tactile tools children can use to help themselves regulate their emotions and return to their window of tolerance.

These might include the following:

- Glitter jar
- Puffer squeeze ball
- Play dough
- Kinetic sand
- Timer
- Expandable ball.

Key 5 Teach children about the safe space

HAPPY ANGRY NERVOUS JEALOUS

DISGUSTED SCARED CRY LOVING

CONFUSED SHY TIRED DISSAPOINTED

All the children and young people will need to be taught about the safe space and why it is such a helpful and essential intervention for our wellbeing. **Why do we need this? what does it help us to do? What are the resources in the area and how do we use them? When and why?** Spending some time as a whole class to reinforce the purpose and practicalities is obviously an essential.

Key tools and strategies

The following tools and strategies are all worth considering in order to support the development of the space and intervention and hopefully increasing your repertoire of key resources which can effectively be used to foster the overall wellbeing of the children and young people you nurture and support, including those refugee children who may be experiencing significant levels of anxiety and distress as they transition into their new school context. Again, it's important to note that these are all very practical, simple strategies which all of us can take use of and incorporate into our toolbox of wellbeing.

It is also imperative that we do not presume that all children and young people will respond in the same way to each of the following tools and strategies. We can teach the strategies; we can model them and share them in the wellbeing curriculum or PSHE lessons whilst also reinforcing the fact that what works for one person may not work for another. Ultimately, key to this is to find out what works for you on an individual basis.

Moving from hyper-arousal to the Window of Tolerance

The power of best breathing

Our breath is an essential in terms of regulating emotions, especially when used with movement. However, not all children will respond well to using breathing techniques. If you think a focus on breathing may be useful to the child, then consider how you can build in some exercises as a proactive measure, *e.g.*, at the start of every school morning and afternoon, or at home before they leave for school or as part of the regular routines in your safe space.

Breathing balls

Cheap breathing balls are very useful and readily available. As children breathe in, the ball expands. As they breathe out the ball closes. *They can repeat as necessary.*

Diaphragmatic breathing

This is also known as belly breathing or abdominal breathing. The belly rises on the in-breath and lowers on the outbreath. This allows effective use of oxygen as it reaches the lower parts of the lungs. Children can practise by placing a hand on their belly and feel the movement. A younger child could practise by lying on their back with a soft toy on their belly - giving the toy a ride as the belly goes up and then lowers.

Progressive muscular relaxation *(PMR)*

This involves tensing and releasing different parts of the body, usually in a systematic way. Tensing on the in-breath and releasing on the outbreath. Caution is needed for high blood pressure or for areas of recent surgery/injury. Research shows that the muscles are less tense following PMR and the proprioceptive sites in the body give feedback to the brain that the body is calmer. It is also useful as it is tangible *(the physical nature of tensing and releasing)*. For younger children they could do a whole-body tense and release, such as pretending to be a robot and then changing to a ragdoll.

Tracing and breathing

The child or young person can draw a shape on a piece of paper. As they breathe slowly in and out they continue to trace the shape without lifting the pencil from the paper.

Visualisation tools and ideas

Provide a range of scripts for visualisation and work with individual children to make up their own scripts for example:

Picture yourself:

- **Gathering the emotions, scrunching them up,** and putting them into a box
- **Walking, swimming, biking,** or **jogging** away from painful feelings
- **Imagining your thoughts as a song or TV programme you dislike, changing the channel or turning down the volume** – they're still there, but you don't have to listen to them.

Weighted blanket

Deep pressure stimulation of the body gained from use of a weighted blanket can increase the release of the feel-good neurotransmitter serotonin in the brain.

Music to soothe

Using the sense of hearing with rhythm can relax both the mind and body. It can be used to accompany breath work, movement and/or PMR. You can grade the music from a higher tempo to lower tempo to gradually regulate.

Personalise this for the child or young person - some people like **the sound of the sea, a stream, a crackling fire, blackbirds,** etc.

54321 GROUNDING

Using the 5 main senses for bringing attention –
5 things they can see;
4 they can feel;
3 they can hear;
2 they can smell (or imagine);
and
1 they can taste (or imagine)

is a very helpful grounding strategy and easy to teach and model to children.

Sensation or feelings wall

A sensation or feelings wall is an area you can create in the safe space with words that describe sensations of feelings. This can be helpful as language is difficult to access when we are dysregulated, but a child could use the visuals and point to the sensation they feel in the body. Remember that the '**language of the brain stem is sensation**.'

Self-reflection sheets/feelings diaries/ calm corner folder

In the personalised folder you can make up for each child, everything can be laminated for easy use and re-use. It can be clipped on a clipboard and hung on the wall with a 3M hook. On the top section of the inside of the file folder, you can have a blank body outline and thought bubble where children can label their physiological feelings and write their thoughts. **Providing some key questions is also helpful:** *How am I feeling? What happened to me? What is my body doing right now? what would help me?*

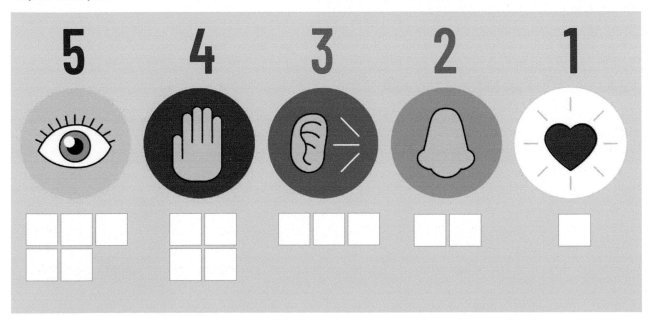

Understanding and **Supporting**
Refugee Children and **Young People:**
A Practical Resource for Teachers, Parents and
Carers of Those Exposed to the Trauma of War

HOW I AM FEELING WORKSHEET

	HAPPY	SHY	DISSAPOINTED	CONFUSED	NERVOUS	SAD	SCARED	ANGRY
Please tick the **emotion you feel** in the **column** and **weekday**								
MONDAY MORNING								
AFTERNOON								
TUESDAY MORNING								
AFTERNOON								
WEDNESDAY MORNING								
AFTERNOON								
THURSDAY MORNING								
AFTERNOON								
FRIDAY MORNING								
AFTERNOON								
SATURDAY MORNING								
AFTERNOON								
SUNDAY MORNING								
AFTERNOON								

Please sum up how you felt during the week

Calm Down Kit
Do you need calm down kit ideas?

A Calm Down Kit will vary in size based on what requirements it need's to fulfil. Some are just in pencil cases, others will be in small boxes or containers. Think of things that may help you and make a list using some of the suggestions here that should go into a calm down kit.

WHAT TO INCLUDE IN A CALM DOWN KIT for **children** and **young people**

There are lots of different things that can be included in a calm down kit, and obviously, it needs to be tailored to the age and requirements of the child(ren) that it is designed to help. **Here are a few suggestions of things you can put in a calm down kit for anxious children and young people:**

- Ear phones
- Eye mask
- Music
- Stress balls
- Play dough or silly putty
- Book
- Crayons
- Fidget items
- Small blanket
- Stress ball
- Notepads
- Pillow
- Puzzle
- Electronic devices
- Putty/plasticine
- Dry erase markers/board
- Gum
- Building bricks

- Activity books: dot to dots, mazes, word searches, I Spy printables
- Stickers
- Colouring books
- Stickers
- Cuddly toys
- Timer
- Books to read
- Tissue paper to rip
- Visual stimulation such as a kaleidoscope or an hourglass
- Whistle, harmonica, party blowers, or similar small wind instrument - To encourage children and young people to breathe out. Also, making music is a great way to release a variety of emotions.

Moving from hypo-arousal to the Window of Tolerance

Our breath is an essential in terms of regulating our emotional state and level of arousal.

Anything that stimulates the senses can be included in a list of strategies/resources that proposes to do this for a child or young person.

Sensory tray

Our sense of smell is the fastest way to the thinking brain. Making a sensory tray with a range of different smelly objects can be a fun activity – lavender, basil, soap, handwash *etc*.

Chewy, crunchy food

Crunchy foods wake us up because we have to work harder to consume them, and that satisfying crunch engages the ears as well. Like crunchy foods, chewy snacks can help a child feel more alert simply because of the effort it takes to consume these foods.

Use of sensory rain stick bottles

Rain stick bottles use the calming effect of the sound of rain to soothe the child's troubles away and can be made from a huge array of household items such as dried rice, beads, or buttons. Support the child to add their chosen objects to fill around half of the container, secure the lid and then engage with the soothing sounds.

Personalised sensory bags

A sensory bag is a bag which is filled with interesting sensory stimulating materials that allow access to explore without getting their hands messy. They are great for younger children under supervision and also for children who experience sensory overload and steer away from getting their hands *'dirty'* Creating these as part of your safe space intervention and individualising them for each child is an essential.

Sand play

If you have the space then providing a sand play area is also extremely useful. If not, then a mini sand tray will suffice.

PAGE
52

Understanding and Supporting
Refugee Children and Young People:
A Practical Resource for Teachers, Parents and Carers of Those Exposed to the Trauma of War

Hand washing/massage

Using essential oils can allow the children to experience different scents. Use a few drops of the oil and they can massage it into their own hand, or work in pairs to massage a peer's hands. Explore the different scents of the oils and the impact they have, for example lavender is calming, eucalyptus is revitalising and uplifting.

Stress/squeeze balls/slime

Stress balls are excellent tools to relieve stress and release anxiety. They also improve motor skills, loosen muscles, promote blood circulation, and strengthen the hand grip. It is worthwhile investigating a range of these to resource the safe space as they are relatively cost effective, and many children and young people find them easy to use both in the corner and while in the class context.

Calm down jars

To make your own calm down jar, mix glitter glue with hot water, add a few drops of food colouring. Whisk until the glue 'melts' and mixes properly with the water. Next, add additional glitter, whisk vigorously one more time, transfer the mixture into your clear jar, and top the bottle up with water so it's completely full. Allow the water to cool to room temperature before securing the lid with glue to ensure it is properly sealed and won't leak. Shake when you need to calm down.

Feeling the soles of the feet on the floor

Feeling the soles of the feet on the floor whilst sat on a chair and noticing how the body is supported is a key grounding technique. The Soles of the Feet practice enables the individual to divert attention from an emotionally arousing thought, event, or situation to an emotionally neutral part of the body.

Dance and music

The calming effects of music are evident as is the use of dance to express emotion and increase endorphins, so having the opportunity to dance to a tape is something you may also wish to consider for some children as a part of this intervention.

Gently sitting or bouncing on a therapy ball

Gently bouncing a sitting child on a therapy ball offers increased vestibular input and this activity helps to raise a child's arousal levels when they are feeling sluggish or slow. It brings about eye contact with the person in front of them in addition to alertness and awareness of one's own body in space.

In the same sitting position, if the therapy ball is rocked front and back, it enhances the balance and postural control of the child while providing vestibular input.

Slow bouncing or slow rocking on the therapy ball for a period (*specific to each child*) brings about a calming effect on the child. On the other hand, fast bouncing or rocking on the therapy ball brings about alertness in a child.

Bouncing can be done in a distraction-free environment such as the safe space with rhythmic music or rhyme that enhances the child's response to his/her surroundings.

Rocking chair or rocking horse

If you have enough space for this it can really enhance the provision and has similar effects to bouncing on the therapy ball.

Finger tracing - collect a series of labyrinth pictures for children to trace around. They can make up their own folders and also include some Mindful colouring activities if these are considered age appropriate.

Sensory trays/bins

To make a sensory bin/tray all you need is a storage container (*can be as small or as big as you would like*) and material to fill the bin. You can use any of the following: sand, oatmeal, rice, dried beans, dried split peas, lentils, or any combination of these. You can then take small toys such as little people, farm animals, matchbox cars, pompom balls, etc. and hide them in the bin. To find the items you have hidden the child/children can use tools like spoons, shovels, trowels, or forks. This allows them to experience different textures with their hands and to develop skills with utensils.

Additional wellbeing support tools

Alongside a focus on self-regulation, there are a range of other wellbeing support tools that school-based staff can effectively make use of. These do not demand specialist training but will probably need some element of supervision from the school's wellbeing coordinator or child and educational psychologist.

Expressive writing approaches

For those children and young people who are able to write, expressive writing approaches can be very powerful. They can be encouraged to write about their experiences, and specifically their feelings about those emotional experiences as this can help to reduce distressing reactions and improve health overall. There are many creative approaches, which to harness the beneficial effects of music, art and play, and link to the child's own culture simultaneously. Talking and writing about feelings on emotional experience can help to reduce distressing reactions. Thinking about this approach logically, it can be likened to maintaining a journal or daily diary when you write down things you are worried about, things you're happy about and the things you're concerned about. When you reread what you've written it can be helpful to think about where you may have been stuck with an issue or problem, whether or not you need to talk to someone about it, and probably make some effort to try and unpick some of those knots that we all get into when we fixate on certain situations and times.

Tree of life

The tree of life activity emanates from Narrative therapy which suggests that we create stories throughout our lives to make sense of our experiences, and we can carry many stories with us at any one time. Although some can be positive and others negative, all impact our lives in the past, the present, and in the future. The Tree of Life enables people (*specifically our refugee children*) to speak about their lives in ways that are not re-traumatising, but instead strengthen their relationships with their own history, their culture, and significant people in their lives.

The tree is seen as a sacred symbol, which carries significant meanings in both religious and spiritual philosophies. While it symbolises many different things, there are some common themes within multiple cultures.

The Tree of Life commonly represents:

A connection to everything - *the interconnectedness of everything in the universe*

Ancestry, family, and fertility - *the connection to one's family and ancestors*

Growth and strength - *trees stand tall and strong all over the world*

Individuality - *trees are all unique*, with their branches sprouting at different points and in different directions

Immortality and rebirth - *trees lose their leaves and seem to be dead during winter*, but then new buds appear, and fresh leaves unfurl in the spring

Peace - *trees have always evoked a sense of calm*, peace, *and relaxation*

There are many templates available online for this intervention. Children can use any arts-based material to create their Tree of Life and the story is narrated and written down. The adult supporting them in the process will often translate it into their language of choice, and provide the child with a laminated version at the end of the work. Usually there is a focus on one section of the tree each time the child or young person meets with their key adult or therapeutic support worker, to ensure time and attention is given to their experience.

The different parts of the tree that the child creates and contemplates are:

Roots: *where you come from and your family*

Ground: *your present life and day-to-day activities you engage in*

Trunk: *your skills and abilities*

Branches: *your hopes and goals*

Leaves: *important people in your life*

Fruit: *gifts from important people (material and non-material)*

Storms: *challenges*

Creative arts therapists and others who make use of this approach find it invaluable in enabling children and young people to speak about their lives in ways that make them stronger. It can be used with individuals and also with groups of children and young people.

Physical activities

An obvious easy win supporting children and young people is to enable a range of physical activities including exercise, play and being out in nature. We know that keeping fit and healthy and taking exercise increases levels of those happy chemicals called endorphins. Engaging in physical activity can also act as a temporary distraction for levels of anxiety, worry or fear that they may have experienced or are continuing to experience. We can liken this to the experience of what Martin Seligman calls '*flow*' where we are in the moment possibly doing something creative or physical, and our minds are not buzzing with patterns of negative automatic thinking and we're just able to focus on the task or activity in hand. This gives an enormous level of release from ongoing stress.

PAGE
54

Understanding and **Supporting**
Refugee Children and **Young People:**
A Practical Resource for Teachers, Parents and
Carers of Those Exposed to the Trauma of War

Loss and **bereavement support**

Sadly, many of our refugee children and young people will have experienced a significant bereavement which will be contributing to their trauma overall. At a school-based level, there may be access to support for bereavement either on an individual or small group level. The majority of educational provisions now have some form of bereavement policy and interventions to support children and young people experiencing grief and loss.

All we can do at the outset, is to ensure we understand how children and young people perceive and rationalise death. We can also recognise and make use of some simple strategies to effectively support our children at such times.

A child's understanding of death varies depending on their age and stage of development. It is important when discussing grief and loss with a child, that you consider their understanding of the situation, in line with their developmental presentation. For example, if a child is aged 12 but presents with learning difficulties and has an understanding of a much younger child, it is likely that their understanding of death will replicate that of a younger child also.

Another important factor to consider when supporting a child through a bereavement is that their understanding of death will develop as they do. Therefore, although a child at the age of four may be unaware that death is irreversible, they may suddenly appreciate that they will never see their *mother/father/ grandma/uncle* again when they reach the age of seven and will need additional support, almost as if the event had only just occurred.

What might you observe if a **child** is experiencing grief?

- **Social isolation and/or separation anxiety**
- **Friendship difficulties**
- **Physical symptoms** (e.g., headaches, stomach aches)
- **Fluctuation of mood/ 'puddle jumping'**
- **Sleep problems**
- **Reduced concentration**
- **Developmental regression** (e.g., bed wetting).

Cultural factors

The one thing that is consistent across all cultures is that death is seen as a transition for the person who has died. However, the preparation and behavioural expectations of those who are

Understanding bereavement:

AGE	UNDERSTANDING
Up to **3 years**	■ **No understanding of death** (rather a separation) ■ **Explore being and non-being through games** ■ **Can sense adult feelings and require non-verbal communication for reassurance**
3 to **6 years**	■ **Aware that death is different or 'special'** ■ **Unaware of inevitability, universality, and irreversibility of death** ■ **'Magical thinking' can lead to self-blame**
6 to **10 years**	■ **Beginning to understand that death is final** ■ **Sense of morality means they may associate death with retribution for wrongdoing** ■ **May appear outwardly unaffected due to denial**
10 to **12 years**	■ **Understand that death is final and irreversible** ■ **Focus on both biological and emotional aspects of death** ■ **Also, aware that they, too, can die – death is personal, universal, and real**
Adolescents	■ **Adult-like understanding of death** ■ **May inappropriately assume the roles of the dead person**

still alive can vary considerably amongst cultures. Although feelings of sadness and anger are commonly experienced across all cultures, the way in which these are expressed can vary significantly, with social expectations presenting differently in each culture. When you are supporting a child (*and their family*) during a period of bereavement, it is important to remain aware of and sensitive to any cultural beliefs that are held around death. Speaking with the family about their cultural beliefs can ensure that the child does not receive mixed messages about what might happen to the person who has died.

Again, it is important to reinforce the fact that some children and young people will become stuck in their grief and heightened levels of toxic stress. Vigilance is an essential here in order to accurately collate the evidence to provide to specialists who may then need to provide direct input to those who may exhibit more complex grief in the longer term.

Referring **on**

Overall, it is important to maintain vigilance in terms of assessing both emotional and academic progress on an ongoing basis. Engaging and supportive network meetings where staff and parents meet together to discuss progress or concerns is clearly an essential. Where there are concerns about the child's emotional wellbeing it is advised to seek additional support from psychologist or the school's mental health. This may well result in an individualised therapeutic package of support. Alternatively, this might result in a more bespoke therapeutic intervention delivered by staff within the school context.

It is particularly important to highlight the fact that there may be some difficulties in determining underlying reasons for a lack of academic progress in refugee children and young people. We know that sustained sociocultural deprivation has an impact on cognitive development, and sadly, some of our children may have experienced this from birth.

It is also vital to note that the effects of trauma can sometimes be misinterpreted. There is some evidence to suggest other difficulties such as attention deficit hyperactivity disorder or oppositional defiance disorder have similar indicators to those demonstrated by children and young people who have experienced trauma (*Perry, 2002*).

School staff need to be mindful of this when making decisions about children's presenting behaviours or difficulties, giving students time to make relationships and make sense of their environment. Consultation and discussion with the SENCO, mental health lead or education and child psychologist may be helpful to develop appropriate courses of action in the classroom.

It is also possible that some of the issues can be due to cultural differences when refugee children do not understand the norms of UK school context. Mentoring and buddy support systems can be helpful in this instance alongside providing access to that therapeutic adult who can be available to them when they need it and provide a sense of belonging when they can ask for help without fear or shame (*Kia-Keating & Ellis, 2007*).

We also know that sociocultural, deprivation has far-reaching consequences: The stress hormone, cortisol, is well-known to have a number of adverse effects, if produced at high levels for long periods, on parts of the brain that are central to memory and learning and higher order thinking and reasoning (*Gerhardt, 2004*). However, it is also evident the barriers to attainment in the first instance, largely related to the way in which tasks are delivered in the learning environment as opposed to the child's intrinsic ability.

With the right kind of sensitive scaffolding and differentiation it is generally the case that most refugee children can overcome such barriers to learning through accessing mediated learning opportunities which can help them to develop their attention, motivation, impulse control, and abstract thinking.

An **important** point

This chapter has focused on how we can support our refugee children and young people, some of whom will have experienced unusually traumatic events in their lives. While the emphasis is being on what we can all do to support them as they integrate into our schools and communities, it is vital to remember that those who work with trauma – whether they are parents, carers, teachers, or other professionals, can become burnt out over time and potentially victims of vicarious trauma.

It is therefore extremely important that individuals concerned and their staff teams or social contacts, retain a focus on personal wellbeing, self-care and provide access to appropriate supervision, reflection, and relaxation opportunities. The focus of the next chapter will consequently be on self-care for those supporting children and young people.

CHAPTER 4
Self-care for those supporting traumatised children and young people

This chapter **covers**

- Understanding trauma
- The risk of vicarious trauma
- Vicarious traumatisation
- Signs and symptoms of VT
- Managing vicarious trauma
- Your calm plan
- Being the role model
- A key issue to consider at the start of a self-care journey
- Top 6 benefits of self-care
- Types of self-care
  Sensory
  Emotional
  Spiritual
  Physical
  Social
- Time for reflection – the SWOT analysis
- The need for appropriate supervision

PAGE
58

Understanding and **Supporting**
Refugee Children and **Young People:**
A Practical Resource for Teachers, Parents and
Carers of Those Exposed to the Trauma of War

Understanding trauma

In order to understand how best to support traumatised children and young people we must first ensure an understanding of what trauma is and how it manifests itself. We must also be very clear regarding the need to understand the impact of working with trauma on those of us who may be undertaking this role on a daily basis. *There is always a risk of re-traumatisation for the adult supporting vulnerable children and their families*. It is therefore important to recognise the signs of vicarious traumatisation and put in place systems to avoid the worst-case scenario.

In this chapter we therefore focus on the nature of trauma, the risk of vicarious traumatisation, how to manage and pre-empt this, and finally consider a range of self-care strategies, tools and ideas which are entirely practical and user-friendly. It is hoped that this will enable the reader to consider their own self-care plan and provide additional resources and ideas to develop this further and maintain it in the longer term.

Van der Kolk et al., *(1989)* described trauma as '***speechless terror***' and traumatised children may be slow to develop speech or may struggle to find words to describe their trauma or their feelings. Trauma and stress may also affect the capacity to process verbal information and children can struggle to follow complex directions and may experience auditory selectivity so that only part of a verbal communication is heard. As adults, we can often interpret failure to obey directions or to respond to questions as wilful defiance and react punitively, rather than modifying our own communication to match the children's needs.

So, once again, we need to be careful to ensure that our responses and the systems we put in place both in the home and in school ensure these factors are considered. *We must respond appropriately to children and young people who have experienced trauma, stress, and anxiety and who are currently living through the traumatic times of a war.* We need to create safety routines first and to also change our own expectations and behaviours.

We all now know that stress and anxiety disorders are an increasing problem for our children and young people and that we do need to therefore work more at a preventative level to support the development of key skills and strategies to manage such issues. Effective stress management and specifically using relaxation strategies can be highly effective for many children. This is the rationale for including a range of such strategies and techniques in this publication. It is vital that all adults *(teaching professionals and parents/carers/refugee parents/carers)* can and do model these to the children and young people they nurture.

To achieve this, we need to ensure that we know how to engage in effective self-care and how to manage our own stress and anxiety whilst simultaneously understanding the need to respond in a truly trauma-informed way. This has never been more important when we know that children are all experiencing such a stressful social and educational context in these difficult times of war and conflict.

The risk of vicarious trauma

Vicarious traumatisation

Research indicates that professionals often find treating survivors of childhood abuse or trauma stressful, because of survivors, resistance to change, their ways of relating to helpers, and the nature of the work *(Palmer et al., 2001)*. The nature of the work is particularly stressful when it involves listening to detailed descriptions of very painful, often horrific events; it may also involve helpers re-enacting survivors' early experiences of trauma and betrayal with them *(Palmer & Edward, 2001)*.

There is no doubt that hearing and thinking about the stories we may hear as a professional can continue well after the client has left the therapeutic interaction.

Historically, therapists' reactions to client traumas were regarded as either burnout or counter-transference. These days, the term vicarious traumatisation *(VT)* is used to describe therapists' trauma reactions resulting from exposure to clients, traumatic experiences *(Pearlman & Maclan, 1995)*.

VT is defined by Saakvitne et al., *(2000)* as the cumulative transformative effect on the helper of working with survivors of traumatic life events, both positive and negative. VT recognises that working with trauma survivors affects the helper and that we must address the effects in order to protect both helper and clients. VT is unavoidable and is the natural consequence of being human, connecting to and caring about our clients as we see the effects of trauma on their lives *(Saakvitne et al., 2000)*. According to Saakvitne et al., *(2000)* the single most crucial factor in the success or failure of trauma work relates to the attention paid to the experience and the needs of the helper. **We cannot meet the needs of our clients or our children when we are overriding our own.**

Saakvitne et al., *(2000)* explain that inevitably trauma therapists will develop an increased awareness of the reality and occurrence of traumatic events, and this makes therapists more aware of their vulnerability. Safety and security are threatened when therapists become aware of the frequency of traumas, often leading to feelings of loss of control and helplessness. VT can affect how therapists relate to their families, friends, and partners. Furthermore, the therapist may experience changes in esteem for themselves and for others.

MAIN SIGNS and SYMPTOMS

CHEST PAIN
OXYGEN SPO_2 lower
LETHARGY
ANXIETY
PALPITATIONS Racing heart
'Gallops in the chest'
SHORTNESS of breath
ELEVATED Ventricle rate or heart rate
DIZZINESS or syncope fainting

VT impacts on areas of psychological need including safety, trust, esteem, intimacy, and control.

Signs and symptoms of VT also include:

- Emotional numbing
- Social withdrawal
- Work-related nightmares
- Feelings of despair and hopelessness
- Loss of sense of spirituality
- More negative view of the world
- Reduced sense of respect for your clients
- Loss of enjoyment of sexual activity
- No time or energy for yourself
- Feeling that you cannot discuss work with family or friends
- Finding that you talk about work all the time *(cannot escape)*
- Sense of disconnection from your loved ones
- Increased sense of danger *(reduced sense of safety)*
- Increased fear for safety of children or loved ones
- Sense of cynicism or pessimism
- Increased illness or fatigue
- Increased absenteeism
- Greater problems with boundaries
- Difficulties making decisions
- Reduced productivity
- Reduced motivation for your work
- Loss of sense of control over your work and your life
- Lowered self-esteem, lowered sense of competence in your work
- Difficulties trusting others
- Lessened interest in spending time alone
- Less time spent reflecting on your experiences.

PAGE
60

Understanding and **Supporting**
Refugee Children and **Young People:**
A Practical Resource for Teachers, Parents and
Carers of Those Exposed to the Trauma of War

Managing vicarious trauma

The trauma model CSDT *(constructive self-development theory)* for working with survivors of childhood trauma is also a useful model for assisting therapists and trauma counsellors to manage their VT experiences. CSDT suggests that changes in the perceived realities of therapists occur as a result of working with traumatised clients and their stories *(Saakvitne et al., 1996).*

Strategies to manage VT as suggested by Saakvitne et al. *(2000)* **include:**

1. Anticipating VT and protecting oneself:

Protecting yourself includes arranging things ahead of time to anticipate the stress of your work and its impact on you.

Strategies include:

- Awareness
- Balance
- Connection.

A sense of balance is considered to be one of the key components to preserving a sense of identity and overall wellbeing. A healthy balance of work, rest, play, including socialisation with friends and

family is important in decreasing the effects of VT. Furthermore, any activities which assist the individual's personal tolerance levels, for example, journal writing, personal counselling, emotional support from partners, will assist the individual to reconnect to emotions.

2. Addressing signs of VT:

Addressing VT includes those things you do for self-care.

Strategies include:

- Self-care
- Self-nurturing
- Escape.

3. Transforming the pain of VT:

Protecting yourself includes arranging things ahead of time to anticipate the stress of your work and its impact on you.

Strategies include:

- Create meaning
- Infuse meaning in current activities
- Challenge negative beliefs
- Participate in community building.

Although the role of the trauma therapist is undoubtedly the focus here, it is vital to remember that any adult whether professional or a parent or carer, will be at risk of some level of vicarious re-traumatisation. Simply being with someone on a daily basis who exhibits trauma-related behaviours and anxieties, will naturally result in some level of stress and anxiety being transferred.

Therefore, it is important to be aware of the possibility of this transferable range of behaviours and emotions, and to take concrete steps to mitigate it at the earliest opportunity. As stated above, one key element of addressing the signs of vicarious traumatisation is that of self-care. Parents, carers and school-based professionals all need to maintain a level of self-regulation which involves an effective self-care plan which is implemented daily. If we are going to be able to effectively support our children and young people to maintain regulation, we need to keep regulated ourselves.

This is the rationale for developing the following plan. **Your calm plan** is intended to provide a visual reminder as to how to maintain focus most effectively on your own wellbeing. It is simple, straightforward, and

TRAUMA TIREDNESS

Z Z Zz

Your calm plan

Yourself first - Attend to your own needs for calm so that you can share it with your child and remember **you cannot regulate others if you are unregulated**

Observe your breathing and take **deep breaths** when it becomes shallow or tight and **put your hand on your heart and just PAUSE**

Understand that it is **normal** to feel anxious when we are in uncertain times and try to remain hopeful knowing that **this too shall pass**

Regulate regularly and use Grounding, Best breathing, Mindfulness, and Exercise to soothe your nervous system – *practice really does make it better!*

Co-regulate with your child and show them how you do it – **MIRROR ME** - copy my breathing - *'Let's visualise together, lets draw out the worries or dance/jog them out together!'*

Accept yourself in the moment and have some **self-compassion** – you cannot always get it right and it's okay to take some **time out to vent**

Look and learn from what happens, and the mistakes you and others make and be solution focused identifying what **DID** work well or better and problem solving instead of being problem focused

Moderate and manage your self-care plan and adapt and be flexible in the moment knowing that finding your calm daily will only benefit you and yours!

Positives matter so try to find **3 good things** at the end of each day and write them down in a journal to re-read and re-visit at your leisure

Learn to focus only on the things you can control and remember, **it takes practice**

Always remember that **self-care is not selfish** as you cannot pour from an empty cup

Neutralise those **negative thoughts** by reframing them into more effective ones and remember **a thought is not necessarily true – always challenge those negative thoughts**

therefore easy to present to a wide range of people who may wish to develop their wellbeing to effectively nurture their children and the young people they support.

The plan also succinctly summarises much of the advice that follows in this chapter. Again, this is presented in a straightforward, user-friendly way and aims to ensure that the reader can access a range of key tools and strategies which are evidence based and really do work.

Being the role model

It is important to also remember that being able to develop skills of positive thinking is essential if we are to model such behaviours and attitudes to the children and young people we care for.

Here are some ways to think and behave in a more positive and optimistic way:

■ **Identify areas to change.** If you want to become more optimistic and engage in more positive thinking, first identify areas of your life that you usually think negatively about, whether it's work, your daily commute, or a relationship. You can start small by focusing on one area to approach in a more positive way.

■ **Check yourself.** Periodically during the day, stop and evaluate what you're thinking. If you find that your thoughts are mainly negative, try to find a way to put a positive spin on them.

■ **Be open to humour.** Give yourself permission to smile or laugh, especially during difficult times. Seek humour in everyday situations and events. When you can laugh at life, you feel less stressed.

■ **Follow a healthy lifestyle.** Aim to exercise for about 30 minutes on most days of the week. You can also break it up into 10-minute chunks of time during the day. Exercise can positively affect mood and reduce stress. Follow a healthy diet to fuel your mind and body and learn techniques to manage stress.

■ **Surround yourself with positive people.** Make sure those in your life are positive, supportive people you can depend on to give helpful advice and feedback. Negative people may increase your stress level and make you doubt your ability to manage stress in healthy ways.

■ **Practise positive self-talk.** Start by following one simple rule: Don't say anything to yourself that you wouldn't say to anyone else. Be gentle and encouraging with yourself. If a negative thought enters your mind, evaluate it rationally and respond with affirmations of what is good about you. Think about things you're thankful for in your life.

PAGE
62
Understanding and **Supporting**
Refugee Children and **Young People:**
A Practical Resource for Teachers, Parents and
Carers of Those Exposed to the Trauma of War

A **key issue** to **consider** at the start of a self-care journey

A major problem for many of us is the fact that self-care sometimes feels like an indulgence, or worse, a selfish act. This is despite the fact that, as we all know, you have to put on your own oxygen mask before you try to help someone else.

Genuine self-care involves recognising and accepting your imperfections, while also finding ways to improve yourself – compassionately. It also often means making compromises and recognising that no compromise is perfect. For instance, you might be torn between time with loved ones and time at work, or time for yourself and time caring for a loved one. Self-compassion involves managing the best that you can, without criticising or punishing yourself for not doing things exactly the way you imagine you should be doing them.

Key to this is the **rejection** of **any notion of perfection**.

Top **6** benefits of self-care

There are six key benefits to engaging in self-care and these will be applicable to all of us, whatever our level of responsibility in any organisation. If you are a teacher, a psychologist or another professional working in school or you are a parent supporting your own children, you will all need to ensure your own wellbeing first if you are to be fit for purpose in your role.

The benefits are **self-evident**:
1. Improved productivity

If you can prioritise your own needs first and make sure that you don't overextend yourself, then you will be able to make more time for things that really matter and improve your wellbeing. Saying no is very important in this process as it enables you to reject the pull of others who are attempting to prompt you to overstretch yourself. This brings your goals into sharper focus and helps you to really concentrate on what you are doing at any given time.

2. Improved resistance to disease

There is evidence that most self-care activities activate your parasympathetic nervous system (PNS). What this means is that your body goes into a restful, rejuvenating mode, helping it to fortify its immune system.

3. Better physical health

Similarly, with better self-care often comes fewer colds, cases of flu and upset stomachs. Less stress and a better immune system can surely help you feel more physically able and strong inside and out.

4. Enhanced self-esteem

When you regularly carve out time that is only about being good to yourself and meeting your own needs, you send a positive message to your subconscious. Specifically, you treat yourself like you matter and have intrinsic value. This can go a long way toward discouraging cycles of negative thinking, feeling, and behaving.

5. Increased self-knowledge

Practising self-care requires thinking about what you really love to do. The exercise of identifying what makes you feel passionate and inspired can help you understand yourself a lot better. Sometimes, this can even spark a change in career or a reprioritisation of previously abandoned hobbies and passions.

6. More to give

Self-care gives you the resources you need to be compassionate to others as well. This of course, is particularly important and pertinent for anyone taking the role of caring or nurturing for traumatised children and young people – specifically those fleeing war and conflict.

Types of self-care

There are **five** **main categories of self-care** for us all to consider and attempt to fit into our daily routines and activities.

1. Sensory

Sensory self-care is all about helping to calm your mind. When we are able to tune into the details of the sensations all around us, it's easier to live in the present moment. This also enables us to more effectively let go of resentments related to the past or anxieties about the future. When we think about practising sensory self-care, we need to consider all of our senses: *touch, smell, sound, taste* and *sight*.

Most people are more responsive to one sense than the others, so we need to ask ourselves what that sense might be for us.

The **following examples** of **sensory self**-**care** **involve** at least **one sense**, but **often more**.

Sensory Self-Care Ideas

- Cuddling up under a soft blanket
- Going to the countryside and focusing on the smell of the air
- Watching the flames of a candle or a fire
- Feeling and noticing the water on your skin during a hot bath or shower
- Focusing on the movements of your own breathing
- Lying down and listening to music with your eyes closed
- Sitting in the heat of the afternoon sun
- Having a small square of the most delicious chocolate
- Walking barefoot in the grass
- Having a massage with essential oils
- Holding a pet in your arms.

If we **want** to **practise better emotional self**-**care** then we can **consider** some of the **following ideas**:

Emotional Self-Care Ideas

- Keep a daily journal/diary and be honest about your feelings (*additional information on journaling is provided in* **chapters 6 and 7**)
- Write a list of "*feeling words*" to expand your emotional vocabulary
- Make time to be with a friend or family member who truly understands you
- Let yourself cry when you need to as this produces a genuine sense of release and the chemicals needed to self-soothe
- Deliberately encourage yourself to relive and visualise happy times and memories
- Sing along to the song that best expresses your current emotions.

2. Emotional

When it comes to our emotional health, one of the best self-care tips is to make sure we fully engage with our emotions. We may feel tempted to push down or reject/ignore feelings like sadness or anger, but it is healthy to feel them, accept them, and then move on.

It is also important to remember that emotions are not "***good***" or "***bad***" in themselves. We do not need to blame ourselves for the emotions we feel; only how we behave in response to them.

3. Spiritual

Spiritual self-care is not simply about having a particular faith or belief in a God. It is about being in touch with our values and what really matters to us.

MY MEMORIES

Understanding and Supporting Refugee Children and Young People:
A Practical Resource for Teachers, Parents and Carers of Those Exposed to the Trauma of War

Self-Care tips for depression often stress that developing a sense of purpose is vital to our recovery.

We may wish to consider some of the following:

Spiritual Self-Care Ideas

- Keep up a daily meditation or mindfulness practice
- Attend a service, whether it is religious or humanistic
- Read poetry
- Walk in nature and reflecting on the beauty around you
- Make a daily list of 5-10 things that make you feel grateful
- Be creative, whether through art, music, writing or another outlet
- Make a list of 5-10 things that make you feel alive, then ask yourself how you can better incorporate these things into your life
- Say affirmations that ground your sense of self and purpose
- Go on a walk with the sole purpose of photographing or recording things that inspire you and make you feel grateful to be here.

4. Physical

The importance of self-care definitely extends to purely physical aspects of our health. Physical activity is vital not only for our bodily wellbeing but also for helping us to let off steam and it produces the feel-good chemicals we all need in order to maintain emotional wellbeing. **We may wish to consider some of the following Physical Self-Care Ideas:**

Physical Self-Care Ideas

- Dancing or exercise classes
- Yoga
- Football
- Tennis
- Cricket
- Running - independently or as part of a running club
- Cycle
- Go for a walk.

In addition, remember that physical self-care is as much about the things we do not do as the things we do.

We can consider the following ideas:

- Taking a nap or short sleep for just 20 minutes can ensure that we feel refreshed both mentally and physically
- Saying "*no*" to invitations when we are simply too tired to enjoy them
- The option not to do an exercise routine when feeling rundown or lacking in energy
- Committing to 7-9 hours of sleep per night.

5. Social

Finally, social self-care is another category that is important for us all. It might look different depending on whether we are an introvert or extrovert. However, connecting with other people is necessary for our happiness for many of us.

We may wish to consider the following ideas:

Social Self-Care Ideas

- Make a date to have lunch or coffee with a good friend
- Write an email to someone who lives far away from you, but who you miss
- Try to reconnect with someone you like but have not seen in a while
- Consider joining a group of people who share your interest, hobby, or passion
- Stop socialising with those who undermine or disempower you
- Join a support group for people who may struggle with the same things you do
- Attend a class to learn something new and meet new people at the same time.

Time for reflection – the **SWOT** analysis

This chapter is intended to be very practical and user-friendly, providing the reader with some helpful tools and strategies to develop and maintain an effective self-care regime.

As stated earlier, this is of course essential for all of those who are working with or seeking to parent children and young people who have experienced trauma and specifically the trauma of war and conflict.

It may be helpful at this point to take some time to reflect on the kind of skills you may need to develop further and how making use of this publication might help you to do exactly that.

It may be helpful to undertake a **SWOT analysis** in order to identify your current **strengths** both internally and in your home or workplace, any **weaknesses**, or areas you may feel you need additional support with at this time, any **opportunities** to develop your skills and knowledge and any **threats** that might impact negatively on your role and performance and ability to foster post-traumatic growth of our vulnerable children and young people in particular.

Once you have completed this analysis you will probably have a greater understanding as to what you need in terms of support going forward in order to effectively undertake this role. If you do have concerns regarding specific areas such as your understanding of trauma, depression or anxiety and need to develop your skills and knowledge base it will obviously be helpful to discuss this with others in your community group or within the school context.

There are a range of professionals both in and outside of the school setting who can help and support us with any gaps in our knowledge and skill set, and in terms of addressing any psychological needs that we may have. These include the educational and child psychology service, the school's mental health lead, the safeguarding lead, and special educational needs coordinator amongst many.

The **need** for **appropriate supervision**

Most importantly, we all *(parents and professionals alike)* need to feel safe in delivering any small group interventions or in undertaking any one-to-one work with traumatised children and young people, and the way in which you do this initially is *always to access support from someone who can help you to process your own responses, reflect on your practice and ensure that you are always responding in the most ethical and appropriate way*.

For many parents and carers this may well involve accessing support groups via local networks, which are frequently run by volunteers with the additional support of a therapist or trauma-informed psychologist.

For the psychologists and those delivering more specialised therapeutic interventions, however, there is clearly an ethical approach to be taken which involves being very clear about setting up regular supervision sessions or peer group support sessions where you can discuss any of your concerns and identify needs for future professional development. This is essentially about keeping both yourself and your clients safe.

STRENGTHS
Your advantages

WEAKNESSES
Areas for improvement

OPPORTUNITIES
Situations to apply your advantages

THREATS
Where you are at risk

CHAPTER **5**

The role of refugee parents/carers

This chapter **covers**

- Challenges for refugee parents
- The power of language for communication
- Top tips for creating successful two-way communication
- Educating through partnership
- Ideas for ensuring that refugee parents become educated partners
- Group support for refugee parents/carers
- Working to support individual parents/carers
- The trauma of life events
- Understanding anxiety
- Understanding post-traumatic stress and intrusive memories
- Understanding avoidance
- Sadness and bereavement
- Irritation, anger, and guilt
- Difficulties with working memory and concentration
- Sleeping problems
- Physical symptoms
- Social relations
- Self-care for the carers

PAGE
68

Understanding and **Supporting**
Refugee Children and **Young People:**
A Practical Resource for Teachers, Parents and
Carers of Those Exposed to the Trauma of War

Challenges for refugee parents

There are a range of personal and practical challenges we may meet in terms of attempting to build positive relationships with newly arrived refugees.

For many refugees, the demanding realities of adapting to a new culture, new workplace, school, or home will often force families into survival mode, and this may well last for some years after they arrive in their new country. There may be difficulties in accessing appropriate childcare and navigating transport systems particularly in terms of getting children to school. Attendance at meetings with school staff may also be difficult due to having to work shifts or manage irregular working hours.

Many refugee elders worry about losing family unity and influence (*i.e., a loss of control*) once their child goes to school. Families also may have experienced prior racial and ethnic discrimination and multiple personal losses, which can increase their wariness about building new relationships (*Hughes & Beirens, 2007*).

Ideas to build strong relationships with refugee families include:

How to build strong relationships with refugee families

Sociocultural conversations conducted in the home or community where family members and educators share stories, traditions, hopes, and dreams as well as fears and worries for their children entering the new educational system.

Collaboration with trained community navigators, who themselves were refugees, to build understanding of differences that require new adjustments at home and school.

Community and home visits to meet families in their own homes or a venue of their choice during non-school hours.

Meetings scheduled at times that demonstrate an understanding and value of family routines, religious practices, work schedules, and other cultural traditions.

A prominent map of the school with staff pictures that indicate where each person is located and that portrays their role at the school.

Administrators who personally plan time to get know each newcomer family and who explain the purpose of formal and informal school events such as coffee mornings or training opportunities.

School events where children invite family members to participate in sports competitions, art/dance/music events or activities, talent shows, local community clean-ups, public murals, or gardening.

Recognition that providing childcare where a child is taken away to another room may not be comfortable for families who would rather keep their young children close by.

The **power** of **language** for **communication**

It is always vital to maintain two-way communication in which both individuals have an equal voice. This means that they have the same opportunities to send, receive and share information, concerns, insights, or impressions. Some of the communication difficulties which present themselves when working with refugee families and children are a direct result of the need to understand cross-cultural communication styles (*Leung et al., 2008*).

When their English is limited, this can reduce confidence in engaging with school staff in particular. They will be left with the feeling that they have little that they can actually contribute, and this is particularly the case when they are asked to meet staff without the benefit of appropriate translation services. This can be extremely uncomfortable and disempowering (*Chu & Wu, 2012*).

We know that children typically learn English faster than their parents or others who might be regarded as elders and their home communities. This can create inconsistent family dynamics where the child or young person appears to have a greater level of autonomy or control. There can also be some difficulties in terms of maintaining family systems in which the roles can seem to be shifting quite considerably at times. Sadly, it is also the case that there are times when a child or young person may be asked to translate for a parent in a meeting and potentially get it wrong *i.e., produce an inaccurate translation* (*Turney & Kao, 2009*).

What is essential is that all educational professionals who work with refugee children and their families access additional training and gain an appropriate knowledge base of how trauma affects individuals both emotionally and physically. This enables effective communication and the development of positive and enabling relationships. Sadly, where staff do not have this level of understanding or skill set, this can result in negative experiences for the refugee parents and children. It is also the case that negative experiences prior to arriving in the host country can lead to fear and anxiety and reduce the level to which the refugee child or adult can communicate in the classroom context and during face-to-face meetings (*Roy & Roxas, 2011*).

TOP TIPS | Top tips for creating successful two-way communication include the following:

- ◼ Translation of all critical school brochures, forms, and policies into both written and verbal (*e.g., video or tape-recordings*) formats so as to overcome literacy issues
- ◼ Multiple formats for communication, such as phone calls, videotapes, e-mails, text messages, TV bulletins, personal contacts, a community buddy system, a designated school-home liaison officer who is fluent in the family's language, among others
- ◼ Critical documents or forms that need to be signed and returned to the school are sent home on distinctly coloured paper
- ◼ Printed and laminated cards with a contact number and directions to the school that family members can easily show to a bus or taxi driver
- ◼ Preparation of families before meetings to explain the purpose of the meeting, what will occur, who will attend, the need for their input, and to get a list of the questions they would like to ask
- ◼ Trained refugee liaison officers who can be contacted by families in their native language when there are questions or concerns about their child or school
- ◼ Collaboration with community service agencies that offer English learning opportunities to see if classes can be offered to family members at the school during school hours
- ◼ Professional development for educational professionals on effective communication strategies that can help overcome reluctance, gain trust, and appropriately respond to strong emotions.

PAGE
70

Understanding and Supporting
Refugee Children and Young People:
A Practical Resource for Teachers, Parents and Carers of Those Exposed to the Trauma of War

Educating through partnership

Refugee parents and carers will feel more confident that they can contribute to any meeting in which shared decision-making is undertaken if they feel that they have the skills and background information. We know that when school staff and parents generally collaborate together it is usually in the best interests of the child or young person and produces the best outcomes for all involved. This also enables a consistent approach and shared understanding between home and school as to what the expectations are for both the family, educational professionals, and the children themselves (Miller et al., 2014).

These positive partnerships can also be effective in supporting refugee parents and carers in learning a range of unfamiliar legal and educational concepts and language. It is also generally the case that the families will particularly appreciate the efforts made to ensure their understanding of classroom teaching approaches, assessment and performance expectations and welcome new ideas for how to help their child at home (Hope, 2011).

It is also helpful to ensure an understanding of cultural attributions about disability and to dispel these at the earliest opportunity, understanding how these can be deeply rooted in shame and guilt *(Leung et al., 2008)*. Variations in authority structures across cultures, especially in regard to schooling, also need to be clarified *(Turney & Kao, 2009)*. While parents and carers in many western countries have important legal authority and must be consulted in almost all educational decisions, this type of authoritative advocacy is not familiar to some refugee families. Finally, limited access to education and English language ability are other crucial factors to consider when helping refugee parents engage in educational decision-making.

Ideas for ensuring that refugee parents become educated partners include:

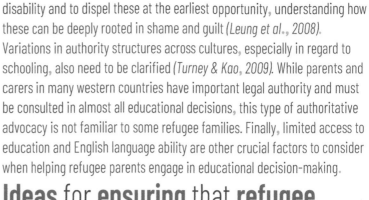

- Access to trained community liaison workers who know how to greet families, put everyone at ease, and explain complex legal concepts and school policies
- Instruction about the UK education system including systems for providing for those with identified special educational needs
- Opportunities for family members to experience school lessons through school visits, video clips of their child that are sent home, or group demonstrations
- Homework assignments that provide a non-threatening way for students and family members to interact or work together on fun, easily completed projects
- Clear explanations of all marking policies and rewards and sanctions systems
- Use of graphs or charts to visually display a child's progress over time
- Family field trips to build knowledge of resources outside of their local community and to strengthen social networking
- Adult classes held at the school on topics such as understanding mental health needs and support, using the library, sporting facilities, use of laptops and career planning
- Information regarding grants or bursaries for family members to attend training, workshops, or courses with the expectation that they would then share their new knowledge with others
- School and community professionals and refugee leaders collaborating as catalysts for change on critical community issues *(e.g., better lighting, new bus routes, more police protection)*.

Group support for refugee parents/carers

Another way of supporting refugee families at the outset is to establish parent support groups. This is an established practice in many countries across the world and a good example of community psychology intended to empower the most vulnerable.

Support groups can be arranged and organised for various groups of refugee families, both those with younger and older children and specific to their first language. Very often groups will be run by an established voluntary community organisation and supported by local authority psychologists such as educational and child psychology services who understand both the educational context and developmental psychology and mental health. An interpreter also can be incorporated into the group so as to ensure and promote effective communication between all involved. In many instances, the services will be provided via local authorities and funded centrally.

The aims of the parent support groups usually include:

- **To give refugee parents an opportunity to share their experiences of raising children and living in the UK;**
- **to learn from one another and offer mutual support;**
- **to help refugee parents support their children's early learning and development;**
- **to gain knowledge and understanding of the English system and services available.**

Parents are usually invited to contribute to the planning of the topic areas to be discussed in the groups.

Each group is different but would generally include the following areas:

- *Aspects of child development*
- *Behavioural difficulties*
- *Play and learning in the home*
- *Dealing with children's sleeping and eating difficulties*
- *Coping with anxiety*
- *Managing flashbacks and intrusive thoughts*
- *Bereavement issues*
- *Coping with cultural bereavement (Eisenbruch, 1991)*
- *Understanding and managing the asylum-seeking process*
- *Maintaining confidence and self-esteem*
- *Supporting parents who suffer from mental health difficulties*
- *Understanding how to support each other and maintain wellbeing*
- *How to ask for an assessment of a child's special educational needs or mental health needs*
- *Understanding the roles of various professionals in the school and psychology services and how they can help refugee families in particular.*

Working to support individual parents/carers

Alongside providing a welcoming context in both the school and local community, psychologists and education professionals also are able to provide a range of interventions to support refugee parents and their children. Most importantly, the need for psychological input and support is widely recognised as being necessary for many. However, it is important to note that this will be bespoke to each individual given the fact that no two refugees can be considered exactly the same.

Some will be more traumatised than others and require a more specialist therapeutic intervention or programme of support, whilst others may simply need the experience of nurture and getting back into a routine and more normal way of life.

However, all refugee families will benefit from support to effectively navigate the trauma of war and their experiences, particularly in terms of being emotionally available to their own children. Many will have concerns regarding the impact of trauma on their children, how to manage heightened levels of stress and anxiety, how to support their child who may be suffering a bereavement and separation anxiety. Also, how to deal with the everyday issues of sleeping difficulties, flashbacks, and a lack of focus and attention which may mitigate against the child accessing learning in the school context.

The following sections therefore provide some practical advice for refugee parents which emanates from evidence-based practice and will hopefully dispel the myths and stereotypes they may have developed alongside increasing levels of confidence that they can and will be able to engage in post-traumatic growth with their children.

PAGE
72

Understanding and Supporting
Refugee Children and Young People:
A Practical Resource for Teachers, Parents and Carers of Those Exposed to the Trauma of War

The trauma of life events

As adults, we can underestimate the extent to which children think about or the extent to which they continue to react to traumatic experiences long after the event. It is also difficult for refugee parents or carers to acknowledge the intensity of the child's reactions, because they themselves may also be experiencing post-trauma symptoms, and want to ensure that their child can recover as quickly as possible. In essence, they simply cannot bear to see how much the child may be suffering. There can be a tendency to think when a child is happy or appearing to be happy, that they are okay, that their worries and concerns are gone and that they have forgotten all about the traumatic experiences they might have come through.

The level of helplessness that a parent or carer may experience cannot be underestimated. Alongside attempting to support their own child, they will also have to be cope with their own reactions, and when a child is presenting as anxious or overwhelmed this may transfer to a parent or carer and remind them of what they went through too.

There is a tendency to try to dismiss or minimise the whole situation as a means of gaining a level of control or autonomy. Parents might say to a child that they are safe now, that they just have to forget the things that they have experienced. Sadly, like dismissing difficult emotions or feelings, this merely compounds the situation.

It would be wonderful if we could simply forget and move on, but this is not the way the trauma works in our minds or in our bodies. Children often need help and support to take control of painful memories that they are storing. Not taking the time to process these memories, to talk about them and feel safe in doing so, will lead to further problems and more significant mental health difficulties along the line. If we try to suppress these memories, to forget them and minimise them, this will not work. What will happen is that they will continually come back and leave a child (*or adult*) feeling helpless.

We know that children will experience war in many different ways and that these will often differ from the experiences of the adult trying to keep them safe and

TOP TIPS

For this reason, the next sections will focus on specific reactions to trauma and traumatic life events and provide advice for parents and carers on how best to support their children.

- Keep communication open and direct
- Having honest conversations is the best way to support children and young people
- Talking about difficult issues with those that love you is much easier as the child feels safe and nurtured
- Do not dismiss any concerns or worries as this simply makes the whole situation worse, particularly if a child or young person hears about it from others as this undermines trust
- Remember that children will pick up signals from you without asking questions so be careful as to how you present to them
- Tell children that if we talk about our worries this will help us cope better in the future
- Always listen for the child's voice, consider their views, and respond once you have processed them

- You can encourage them to answer your gentle questions – what do you think about that? Did you think a lot about that? I have been thinking a lot about this...Is there anyone else that you are thinking about right now?
- Avoid mixed messages. For example, saying everything is fine when the child can see that it is not by your demeanour as this causes additional stress
- Remember that children take in a lot of information and often do so when adults are talking together – so be careful regarding what you want them to actually hear at any given point in time
- Explain things in a warm, loving, and nurturing way as this helps them to regulate their emotions
- Avoid unnecessary periods of separation and let your child know that you are going away or leaving them for a brief period ahead of the time in order to reduce anxiety
- Remember physical closeness and contact produces happy chemicals that help a child or young person to relax and feel safe and loved.

effectively parent them. War and conflict are terribly frightening and distressing to children and young people, putting the brain into a state of alert in order to warn the body that needs to be mobilised in the face of danger in order to survive. Younger children will attempt to stay close to their parents in order to gain a sense of security at this time and all children will use up a huge amount of energy and simply trying to survive. Sadly, many will have learnt to successfully suppress their reactions and responses in order to survive but this can be damaging in the long term even if it lessens the psychological pain in the first instance.

The way in which we can and sometimes do protect ourselves is to view the situation as unreal, it is as if we can step back and look at it from outside, taking a helicopter view rather than feeling as if we are actually in the situation itself. This kind of numbness may last a considerable time once we have left the danger and trauma, but it is particularly important that we engage with children in order to encourage them to understand exactly what has happened to them.

They need to be given simple, clear, and accurate information by the adults in their lives as this helps to organise their thoughts and understand what is actually happening to them and why they needed to leave their homeland. It is vital that their responses are normalised so that they can see and understand that what they are going through is quite natural and something to be worked through. This can be quite challenging and emotionally draining for the adults concerned.

This is why it is also so important for refugee parents and carers to gain additional support and help from their local community groups, from staff in schools, and from, where appropriate, psychologists who work with both children and adults in order to promote wellbeing and post-traumatic growth.

For this reason, the next sections will focus on specific reactions to trauma and traumatic life events and provide advice for parents and carers on how best to support their children.

Understanding anxiety

We know that when we are exposed to danger, our brains become more alert. There could be a sign or signal of danger and sometimes these can be harmless, such as a noise or a slight movement. However, when we are anxious even the smallest signal can seem extremely threatening.

Sometimes a child or young person will also have problems in concentrating on any given task and difficulties in maintaining healthy sleep patterns. There is also the possibility that they may develop a genuine fear of losing someone close to them and find it difficult to leave a parent or carer for fear that they might disappear or be killed or die. This separation anxiety can be common amongst refugee children, and parents need to be very aware of this and understand how the anxiety presents itself and also the very real need that the child may have to be close to their parent or carer, keeping them in their vision at all times.

Living with this level of anxiety and fear can be extremely overwhelming and exhausting for a child or young person. Their biggest fear is obviously that something is going to happen to their parent or carer, but they may also try to cover this up, deny it or engage in what we call 'masking'. This in itself can be problematic because pretending to be okay when you are not can leave you at risk of subsequent meltdowns, for example, at the end of the school day after having presented as relatively calm and assured, the child might return to the home and simply explode with rage, tears, or aggressive behaviours.

TOP TIPS

- Be kind, patient and understanding when the child displays anxiety
- Remember anxiety can display itself as aggression or difficult behaviour so be aware of this and do not punish the child for displaying symptoms of trauma and anxiety
- Learn how to co-regulate with your child, using tools such as deep breathing, five finger breathing, visualisation and mindfulness techniques being careful to note what does and does not work for each individual
- Draw out a visual timetable for each day in order to prepare the child ahead for what is going to happen
- Do not dismiss fears or worries and spend the time talking them through, identifying where they may have gone wrong in their thinking and then helping them to problem solve
- Help the child or young person to develop their own worry plan, making use of formats and resources from chapter 6 and 7 of this publication.

PAGE
74

Understanding and **Supporting**
Refugee Children and Young People:
A Practical Resource for Teachers, Parents and
Carers of Those Exposed to the Trauma of War

Understanding post-traumatic stress and intrusive memories

It is a fact that the most significant and dangerous situations a child or young person has experienced will be the ones that they remember with the greatest ease and most frequently. The reason why this happens is because the brain is attempting to help us become aware of new dangers. The substances released in the bloodstream when we are afraid or distressed will clearly have an impact upon our working memory.

It is also the case that when we are exposed to very frightening and overwhelming situations, the memories of these events can be permanently etched into our minds. They become stored up deep in our memory and will include visual aspects, sounds, tactile sensations, smells, and tastes.

These can then reappear at a later stage in the form of really distressing memories. These kinds of flashbacks result in the individual virtually reliving the event and anything that reminds us of it can trigger the situation. This can be the smallest things such as a specific smell or sound which retriggers that reliving of the memory.

The problem for the child or young person is that these memories can return uninvited, disturbing their ability to concentrate, focus and engage in cognitive tasks. This also has an impact on the child's ability to learn new things in the classroom or social context. What is vital is that they learn strategies to control these kinds of intrusive memories whilst recognising that thoughts, feelings and memories will pop into their minds occasionally many years into the future.

TOP TIPS

- Do not be frightened to talk to your child about the worst things they have experienced as this helps them to organise their memories so that they become less overpowering and less distressing
- Listen, confirm their experiences, and gently question them in order to gain more details and follow up on their concerns
- Remind them that the danger is over now, and they are safe on a continual basis
- Remember that when we talk about painful memories this may initially give rise to more nightmares and heightened levels of anxiety, but this will reduce over time
- Give children the opportunity to express their emotions and feelings through drawing and writing activities including journaling, painting, and making memory books as described in chapters 6 and 7
- Provide additional support for children who have a less developed vocabulary to find words to express their feelings and fears
- Empathise with the child and also share your own feelings in a safe way. For example, the worst thing for me was, I wish I could have *etc.* This will show that you can put yourself in their shoes and also affirm for them that what they are experiencing and feeling is quite normal
- Work together on creating a special storybook of your own experiences as a family so that everyone involved can give their views and create a shared narrative together
- Allocate some special worry time on a daily basis so that the child or young person can talk about their fears, worries and any intrusive memories that they may be having
- Go through each worry in turn and help them to see why their concerns may not become a reality, *i.e.*, these are the reasons this will not happen
- Help the child to make use of their worry time and if they worry outside of this period of time, to either remind themselves to wait to worry or simply write it down on a post-it note which they can go back to and consider later when they are having their worry time
- Remember that practice makes perfect and if we continually challenge our irrational thinking, the thoughts will ultimately stop automatically as everything we do becomes automatic if we do it often enough.

Understanding avoidance

It is also common for a child to avoid anything connected with the traumatic experience in order to attempt to manage the heightened levels of anxiety. This might include specific situations, people, or reminders such as specific smells sounds, memories or thoughts. All of these can prompt children and young people to try and avoid a specific situation. The problem with this is that when they withdraw from their usual everyday activities their lives will become more restricted. In a school context they are also more at risk of developing emotionally based school avoidance. This is because they will not want to be away from their parents or caregivers but also retreat from anything that might have been a normal routine such as going to school, socially interacting with members of their peer group, and engaging in curriculum activities.

This kind of avoidance may result in them becoming hypo-aroused where they can present as totally withdrawn, emotionally unresponsive and very tired and unhappy. They can present as passive and emotionally numb. However, they might also present as hypo-aroused where they are seen to be constantly on the move, overactive and concerned about everything that is going on around them, unable to rest or sit back and simply be in the moment.

It is important to recognise what we can do to support children experiencing this kind of avoidance, which is why many helpful strategies are included in *chapter 3* alongside useful handouts and resources in both *chapters 6* and *7*.

TOP TIPS

- Remember to take things step-by-step and do not rush the child to engage in conversations about their fears and worries
- Provide creative outlets so that they can express how they are feeling in a safe way without the use of language if appropriate
- Work carefully with school-based staff to build a relationship so that the child knows that you feel safe with the adults in that context as this will reassure them and help them to see their new school as a safe space for them
- Help the child to construct their own activity schedule, including daily activities which they find pleasurable, non-threatening and can do with others in the family. These might include going for a walk, watching something funny on the television or on their phones, playing games or creating things
- Play is an incredibly positive way to reduce anxiety for children and young people and needs to be encouraged on a regular basis throughout each day
- Remember happy conversations, positive interactions, play and eating together will all be nourishment for a child's brain development
- Make use of routines which are clearly set out and adhered to on a daily basis. We know routines are good for us in a crisis because they give us stability and structure, and this is particularly true for children and young people who have experienced trauma
- Let the child know that you value every attempt they make and reward them with genuine praise as they take small steps to overcome their anxieties and fears.

PAGE
76

Understanding and **Supporting**
Refugee Children and Young People:
A Practical Resource for Teachers, Parents and
Carers of Those Exposed to the Trauma of War

Sadness and bereavement

Sadly, some of our refugee children will have experienced the death of significant adults in their lives including family members, neighbours, good friends, or others who may have supported them in school or in their local community. Alongside this loss, they will also have lost their home, access to schooling and the sense of security that comes from living a life free from fear of bombings, murder, rape, and abuse.

The loss that a child or young person experiences will be significant. They may present with enormous amounts of sadness, longing, and sorrow.

However, it is important to remember that they may move from sadness to happy or content states quite quickly, where they engage with others and seem to be free from any anxiety. Sometimes we can think of this as '*puddle jumping*'. One minute they may be okay, the next minute they may present as incredibly sad and have a few tears. *It is important to remember that children do grieve, but their grief may be expressed in different ways to what an adult may consider '**normal**' grieving behaviour.*

For example, a child may be crying and needing a cuddle one moment, describing how sad they feel and how much they miss their loved one, and then in the next moment will happily go off to play with their friends.

'*I feel sad that mummy has died, but we are still going to the theme park tomorrow aren't we?*'

As parents and carers, it is important for you to gain an understanding as to how to help the children regulate the force of their reactions and feelings, so that they can begin to gain more control and manage them more effectively.

Simply explaining what is happening in terms of any ongoing war, what has happened previously and why the war occurred in the first place, can be a first step to supporting a child to become more regulated in terms of managing these powerful feelings.

TOP TIPS

- ■ Make sure that children have access to their own culture whilst recognising they will open up to new influences when navigating their loss and grief
- ■ Maintain the first language and remember that those who are fluent in their mother tongue tend to be better at understanding words and concepts of a new language, so this is a real strength to build on
- ■ Always acknowledge the losses that the child experiences
- ■ Normalise feelings of loss as being something that we all expect to experience
- ■ Do not get distressed when the child seems to alternate between sadness and joy as this is normal too
- ■ Encourage children to write or draw about the losses, to collect special items for memory books or journals. There are a range of activities and formats in chapters 6 and 7 which you might find helpful for this purpose
- ■ Allocating special time to feel sad or worried can be helpful for a child or young person to manage their loss on a daily basis
- ■ When the child feels overwhelmed by grief teach them how to say to themselves '*I started to think about my loss again but I'm going to stop, put it back in my memory box and bring it out when I have some grief time for myself*'.

Irritation, anger, and guilt

As adults, it is important that we normalise children's anger about what has happened to them and their families. Sometimes they may direct their anger at those they perceive to have started the conflict, engaged in the conflict, or maintained the level of violence towards those that they love within their communities.

They may also express anger towards parents and carers who they think might have let them down or failed them in terms of keeping them safe in protecting them from the situation. This can be difficult for parents to cope with, particularly when the anger is directed at them and the child or young person becomes aggressive, violent, and emotionally distressed. This level of anger will also be further compounded if the child or young person is having problems sleeping, or they are living in substandard accommodation and displaying hyper-arousal behaviours which leave them feeling mentally and emotionally exhausted. Parenting children with heightened levels of irritation and anger is clearly not an easy task.

As human beings, we all have the tendency to blame ourselves for things that we have done, particularly those that we perceive to be mistakes or inappropriate behaviours. It is important to remember, however, that very often we get things wrong and what we think, or feel is not always a fact. Sadly, many of us engage in these negative patterns of thinking, feeling, and behaving which can become vicious cycles and have a negative impact on our mental health and overall wellbeing.

For example, a child may feel that they could or should have saved someone from the bombing, saved someone from drowning or they could have taken other members of the family with them when they escaped the conflict and fled to safety. Feeling such heightened levels of guilt can have a negative impact on their self-confidence and feelings of self-worth. This is compounded by the losses that they have experienced including the loss of their friendship circle, personal belongings, and the position that they might have held in the family group or social contexts.

Again, all of these factors will impact negatively on their level of self-esteem and confidence. It is not uncommon for a refugee child or young person's to describe themselves as feeling worthless simply because they have lost everything. This is why it is so important for parents, carers and those supporting a child or young person's school context, to really reflect upon and celebrate their skills, their strengths, and the extent to which they are valued by all who love them and seek to support them.

TOP TIPS

- Always remember that children are very often angry without realising the reason why so being angry in return is simply counterproductive
- Be clear that taking out anger in any physical way against others is not acceptable
- Remove children from situations where they are becoming angry and provide them with the opportunity to regulate, co-regulating with them until they are in a calmer place
- Do not discuss the issue with the child until they are calm, and you are calm
- Try to provide them with prompts as to what you think causes their anger as this encourages them to talk about their reactions and learn how to cope with it more effectively
- Normalise the fact that we all experience anger
- Teach them to use self-talk when they are beginning to feel overwhelmed or angry - I can deal with this, I can calm down again I have done it before, I can take a deep breath, let it out slowly and feel myself calming down
- Praise the child when they do apologise, use calming techniques, trying to remain in control
- Model ways of responding to situations that make you angry so that they see how it is possible to manage this without resorting to violence or aggression
- Always remember that we can talk it to tame it - an extremely useful mantra to maintain
- Show children that it is quite natural to feel guilty at times and that very often this can prompt us to put things right when we have done something wrong or got something wrong
- Show them how much you love them and value them as individuals and point out all their positive points and characteristics on a regular basis in order to reinforce their self-esteem and confidence.

PAGE
78

Understanding and **Supporting**
Refugee Children and **Young People:**
A Practical Resource for Teachers, Parents and
Carers of Those Exposed to the Trauma of War

Difficulties with working memory and concentration

It is not surprising that children and young people who have experienced trauma and are continually trying to navigate intrusive memories, will also present with difficulties in concentration and memory. When you are in a survival mode and fearful of everything around you including your future, it is not surprising that you will struggle with both memory and concentration, particularly when asked to engage in the learning process in school context.

TOP TIPS

- Using worry time can help the child to manage intrusive thoughts or memories which may impact on concentration
- Give the child bullet point lists to aid memory
- Make use of lists on their mobile phones to help them if this is useful and accepted within the classroom
- Create a buddy system so that other children in the family or in the classroom can prompt the child at the start of each activity and check in on them at each stage to make sure that they have understood and assimilated to the information necessary to complete the task
- Make sure that staff and school give the child frameworks for activities so that they can tackle them step-by-step without being overloaded and simply have to remember step one first, step two second *etc.*
- Practise simple relaxation techniques that the child or young person can use in the classroom context without being visible to others. For example, grounding the soles of the feet or five finger breathing can be done underneath the table in the classroom.

Sleeping problems

Many children and young people will also experience difficulties in maintaining a good sleep pattern. Sometimes they might have trouble falling asleep and also wake up continually throughout the night. This is due to the fact that their brains are often in a hypervigilant state. This impacts on their ability to reach the deep sleep state that they would otherwise have been able to do had they been relaxed and able to switch off.

TOP TIPS

- Have some talk time before bedtime so that the child or young person can discuss their concerns or worries
- Help to problem solve any concerns and write down solutions if necessary as this will help them to feel calmer before trying to sleep
- Use distraction methods such as counting backwards from 1000 in steps of 7, 5 *or* 1
- Use a breathing exercise when you first breathe normally together for three times and on the third intake the child can hold their breath for as long as they can manage. You can then breathe in and out again three times normally and again repeat the holding of the breath after the third intake. For many this will help them to become drowsy and eventually fall asleep if it is repeated enough times
- Remember that focusing on breathing exercises or your breathing itself will divert attention away from any worries or anxieties or the thoughts that create them
- Remind the child that it is important to take control of memories and get them to imagine they have a remote control which they can use to turn the image or film on and off. Also, to fill the entire screen with the frightening image and then to replace it with a different or more positive one in one corner. They can then visualise this growing bit by bit over the whole screen, pushing the painful memory away and eventually replacing it in its entirety
- Ask them to visualise happy endings, good times, and positive things that they may have experienced during the day, as thinking about these last thing at night will produce less of the anxiety that overwhelms them
- If the child is scared of particular sounds and noises you can help them to pretend that they are listening to them on their mobile phone or on a recording. They can then turn the volume down and edit this memory by creating music for it or anything else that may change the memory of this particular sound.

Physical symptoms

Children and young people may also experience a range of physical symptoms including stomach aches, headaches, or other pains in various parts of their bodies. They might also become more tired than previously due to the levels of hypervigilance they engage in in their effort to push away any painful or distressing memories or flashbacks. These symptoms tend to reduce over time and rarely need advice from a doctor. However, should they continue for a prolonged period of time then it would clearly be advisable to seek support.

TOP TIPS

- Urging them to express themselves in creative ways including writing, painting or physical exercise might help them to reduce some of these physical symptoms
- Talking them through their anxieties can also reduce the physical symptoms and show them that they can take control of these memories by discussing them with a trusted adult.

Social relations

Sadly, for many refugee children and young people, they will experience some level of isolation as they will have lost face-to-face contact with their friends. Keeping connected via social media is an option that many will make use of quite effectively. However, for many, this will not be a viable replacement for face-to-face contact in the longer term. Some will make new friends and forge new relationships relatively quickly in their new country whilst others may withdraw from engaging with others, sometimes because they are very fearful of having to go through yet another loss at some point in the future. This can be extremely isolating and cause heightened levels of depression and anxiety and is particularly compounded when the young person has lost someone close to them and is mourning that loss.

TOP TIPS

- Reassure the child that they can still remain connected even though they are not physically with someone else
- Encourage participation in a range of social activities with others but do this very gently, not forcing the child in the initial stages but simply choosing one activity they could do with another child which is not threatening to them
- Discuss any concerns with school staff who may then be able to set up the circle of friends or peer support system for the child which can boost their confidence and create more regular opportunities to socialise and engage with others.

PAGE
80

Understanding and **Supporting**
Refugee Children and **Young People:**
A Practical Resource for Teachers, Parents and
Carers of Those Exposed to the Trauma of War

Self-care for the carers

Chapter 4 focuses on the development of self-care behaviours for those who are engaged in supporting children and young people who are recovering from the trauma of war and conflict. However, it is really important to also highlight the need for the parents and the direct carers of refugee children and young people to look after themselves too.

The best thing that any parent or carer can do is to look after themselves first. This is vital as they will also be experiencing the after-effects of war and feeling extremely vulnerable and stressed as they attempt to navigate a whole new way of life. This can sometimes lead to difficulties in maintaining positive relationships and being able to comfort children effectively and give them the kind of stimulation they need in a transition to a new life. The stress of attempting to be the nurturing and caring adult while also managing this level of anxiety can be overwhelming at times.

Sadly, there is no easy solution here and the best advice is simply to make use of tried and tested self-care strategies, many of which refugee parents and carers have used successfully in the past. These will not be effective for everybody, and some may work better than others. As always, when we are trying to create our own self-care programme, we need to engage in some trial and error and find out what works best for us as individuals.

In the first instance it can be helpful to simply reflect on what worked well for you in the past. We will all have our own repertoire of tools and strategies that help us to calm down and manage stressful situations on an everyday basis. Even though you may be facing or experiencing a greater level of stress and anxiety than previously, this does not have to mean that the strategies you used before will not work now. It can be helpful to take some time to reflect and make a list of all the things that did work well and then consider how you might make use of them in your new life. These might include engaging with others, taking exercise, praying, journaling about your worries or concerns, listening to music or engaging in other creative activities.

In this chapter we have discussed a range of tools and strategies to help children manage a range of difficult situations and it is entirely possible that many of the approaches used successfully with them can also be used by adults too. It can be helpful to go back over the chapter and write down some of the difficulties that you experience with your child and consider the suggestions made for helping them which might also be applicable or useful to you.

What is vital is that you ask for help if you know that you are really struggling with your feelings and responses to the situations you have experienced or are currently experiencing. This is not a weakness. It is a strength. It is also essential as if you do not do this then you will not be fit for purpose in terms of supporting your child or children. Without a proper self-care routine and the additional help you might need to access from a trauma specialist, you will become less sensitive to your child's needs and concerns and become more irritable and angry yourself. So, it is vital that you put on your own oxygen mask first before trying to support or nurture your child.

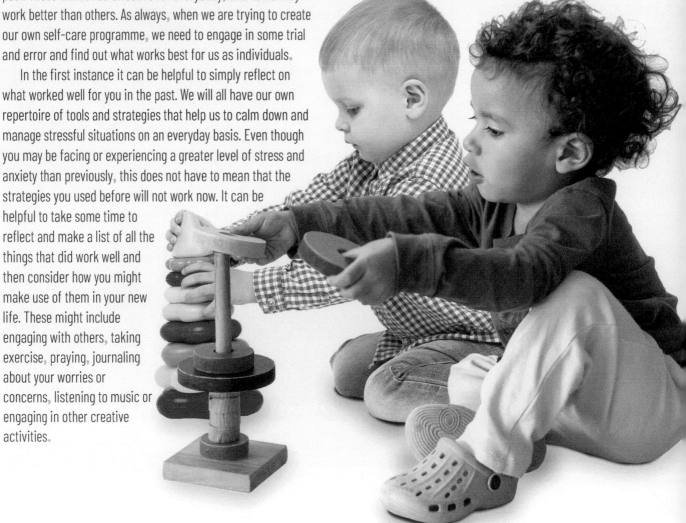

TOP TIPS

- Take regular exercise such as walking, jogging, dancing, or swimming so that you can produce endorphins needed to maintain a well-regulated nervous system

- Timetable in periods of rest when you can simply switch off from social media, the news, and other sources of information

- Use music to self-soothe creating your own calm tapes of pieces of music you know produce or trigger happy memories and connotations for you

- When you start to think negatively stop and think and ask yourself how true is this thought? What is the evidence for it? What is the evidence against it? How can I reframe this into something more helpful and constructive for me?

- Make use of journaling, writing down your innermost thoughts and feelings for 15 to 20 minutes a day as this will help you to put everything into perspective, organising it all and creating a better sense or understanding about what has happened to you and your family

- Writing down what you have learned from your experience is also really helpful, particularly if you can give advice to others going through similar difficulties or situations

- Stay connected with those people who love you and can listen to you and support you as this is good for your emotional wellbeing

- Make the effort to connect with others in your new community, particularly building relationships with others who can share resources, and help you to integrate successfully

- Try to remain hopeful about your new life as this will model positivity to your children and counteract any hopelessness you may all be experiencing at various times

- Join support groups for your refugee community so that you can share ideas, resources and concerns and build strength together.

In conclusion

The emphasis on **self-care** for refugee parents and carers remains a crucial one. There are many tools and strategies that can be used effectively to achieve and maintain wellbeing, and the key is to identify what works best for you and to keep prioritising it via a regular routine. It can be extremely hard to put yourself first, particularly when you have been responsible for nurturing those who are more vulnerable or dependent on you through so much trauma and pain.

However, as stated previously, **self-care** is an essential, it is not selfish, and it is a prerequisite for being able to care effectively for others.

The subsequent chapters in this publication next provide a wealth of tools, strategies, and helpful information to support you in this process.

CHAPTER 6

Handouts and resources for children and young people

This chapter covers

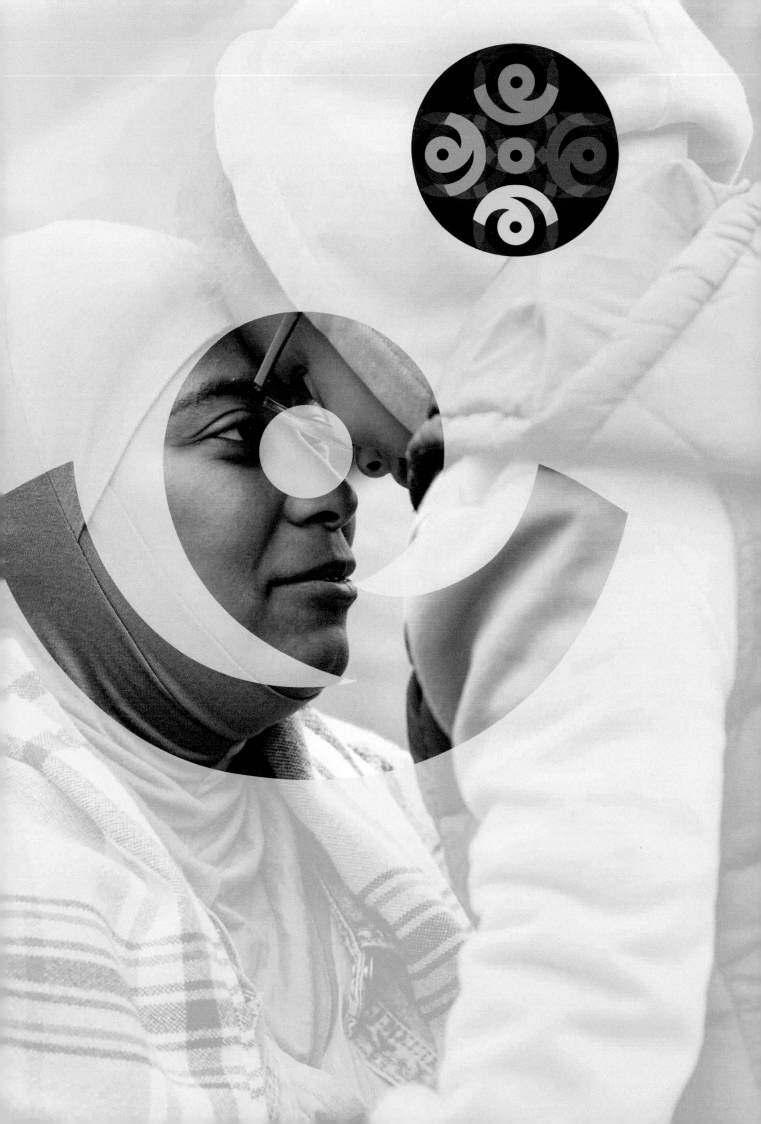

PAGE
84

Understanding and **Supporting**
Refugee Children and **Young People:**
A Practical Resource for Teachers, Parents and
Carers of Those Exposed to the Trauma of War

This chapter presents a range of useful handouts and resources for children and young people.

These can be used in a flexible way with individuals or groups of children and young people and differentiated in many instances by outcome.

For example, if an activity requires a younger child to write their ideas or responses, this can be undertaken by the adult acting as a scribe for them. Some activities can also be self-selected by individual children as part of their individual intervention or support plan.

The handouts and activity sheets are straightforward with easy-to-follow instructions.
It is therefore possible to make use of them without the need for additional instructions other than those that are provided.

The activities include information on understanding anxiety, trauma and feelings, and how to keep safe emotionally and how to develop self-regulation skills and ways of managing worries and make use of tools which ensure post-traumatic growth.

Handouts and activities are as follows:

1. UNDERSTANDING TRAUMA INFORMATION SHEET
2. DEALING WITH TRAUMA REMINDERS INFORMATION SHEET
3. MY CHILLAX PLAN
4. MY JOURNEY HERE
5. MY TIMELINE
6. MY TREE OF LIFE
7. MY MEMORY STONES
8. RECOGNISING FEELINGS INFORMATION SHEET
9. EXPERIENCING FEELINGS IN YOUR BODY
10. FOUR SIMPLE STRATEGIES FOR MANAGING ANXIETY
11. THREE KIND ACTS AND THREE GOOD THINGS
12. POSITIVE REMEMBERING
13. THREE MINDFUL BREATHING EXERCISES
14. PROGRESSIVE MUSCLE RELAXATION
15. THOUGHT TROUBLES
16. THOUGHT CHALLENGING
17. WRITING ABOUT WORRIES
18. MEMORY BOX
19. MY WORRIES ACTION PLAN
20. MY ANXIETY LADDER
21. MY CALM PLACE
22. SLEEP CHECKLIST
23. HOPES AND DREAMS HEART
24. MY HAPPINESS LOG
25. MY WELLBEING AND SAFETY PLAN

1 HANDOUT/ ACTIVITY SHEET

Understanding and **Supporting** Refugee Children and **Young People**
A Practical Resource for Teachers, Parents and Carers of Those Exposed to the Trauma of War

PAGE **85**

Understanding trauma
INFORMATION SHEET

We all experience stress.

School can be stressful.

Arguments with friends and family can be stressful.

Those are normal types of stressors. **Sometimes things happen** that **go beyond normal stress.**

Extremely stressful events are known as **traumas. War** is a **trauma.**

Traumas are usually situations where someone was abused, hurt or killed or thought they could have been.

Traumas can cause a lot of feelings including being **confused, terrified, overwhelmed, helpless, angry,** and/or **numb.**

When faced with a trauma, you go into survival mode and use survival responses like **fight, flight,** or **freeze.**

When you **experience trauma,** especially over and over again, you can get "*stuck*" in survival mode. It can be hard to feel safe. You may feel out of control or that life is out of control.

It can be hard to **trust people** or get **close to people.** You may **get into a lot of conflict** with the people around you. **You can also start feeling like nobody** cares about you.

It is **important to remember** that these are **all normal reactions.**

Stop, think and **reflect** about your own experiences.

Make a list of your feelings and your **behaviours** right now. Then identify a trusted adult you can go to to talk through each item on your list.

Remember that **talking is the best medicine.**
Make your list here:

1

2

3

4

5

6

7

8

9

10

© Copyright TINA RAE 2023

Understanding and **Supporting** **Refugee Children** and **Young People**
A Practical Resource for Teachers, Parents and Carers of Those Exposed to the Trauma of War

Dealing with **trauma reminders**

INFORMATION SHEET

Trauma reminders are things that remind you about the trauma(s).

They can include certain places, situations, people, words, sounds, smells, sensations, or days of the year that remind you of the trauma(s) but are not actually dangerous.

When you experience these reminders, you may feel unsafe or as if you were living through the trauma(s) over again. You may find yourself engaging in behaviours that don't fit the situation or get you in trouble with others. You might also avoid anything associated with the trauma reminder. This can get in the way of your life and the things you like to do.

At times you may have strong emotional reactions to situations that seem unrelated to prior traumatic experiences. But once you are aware of your possible reminders, you can use coping and relaxation skills to manage your emotional reactions better.

3 things I can do **to relax right now**

1

2

3

3 things I can do **to replace the reminders with a happier alternative**

1

2

3

3 people I can talk to **who can help me when I have a reminder**

1

2

3

© Copyright TINA RAE 2023

3 HANDOUT/ ACTIVITY SHEET

Understanding and Supporting Refugee Children and Young People
A Practical Resource for Teachers, Parents and Carers of Those Exposed to the Trauma of War

PAGE
87

MY Chillax PLAN

After traumas happen, you might feel tense, **"*on edge*"**, and anxious. This is because when faced with danger or extreme stress, our bodies release stress hormones to help us survive.

It can be hard to concentrate in school, to sleep, and to feel calm and safe with all these stress hormones floating around our bodies. But there are things you can do to feel more relaxed.

What do you do when you need to chill out?

Sometimes we do things to relax that can cause more problems (*playing computer games instead of studying for a test*) or may not be good for us in the long run (*eating too much*). Are there any down sides to the things you do to relax?

What do you do? Check out the list and then make your own plan.

	MON	TUE	WED	THUR	FRI	SAT	SUN
1. Focused breathing							
2. Progressive muscle relaxation							
3. Guided meditation							
4. Music							
5. Art							
6. Yoga/stretching							
7. Exercise/sports/dance							
8. Relaxation apps							
9. Soothing activities (*taking a warm bath, putting on lotion, wrapping up in a blanket*)							
10. Talking to a friend							
11. Reading							

© Copyright TINA RAE 2023

Understanding
and **Supporting**
Refugee Children
and **Young People**
A Practical Resource for Teachers,
Parents and Carers of Those
Exposed to the Trauma of War

My journey here

Everyone has a different life journey.

For some of us our journey will have been safe, happy and sometimes exciting. But for others their journey may have been very different.

Stop, think and **reflect** on your own journey. Where have you come from and how did you get here?

Use the writing frame

(right) to tell your own story from start to where you are now. You can do this in the form of a letter to someone you love and care about or simply as a descriptive piece of writing that you may wish to illustrate.

© Copyright TINA RAE 2023

5 HANDOUT/ ACTIVITY SHEET

Understanding and **Supporting** **Refugee Children** and **Young People** A Practical Resource for Teachers, Parents and Carers of Those Exposed to the Trauma of War

PAGE **89**

My timeline

Generating a timeline can help us process what has happened to us in our lives.

This line can be *straight, smooth, jagged, curvy* – whatever you feel represents your life.

At the far end of the line, write your **date of birth**. At the other end, **write today's date**. Then map on all the significant events that have happened in your life.

You might want to include drawings or symbols to represent events and you can also discuss how you felt before, during and after certain events with a trusted adult.

This activity can be helpful for all of us when we have experienced loss through a terminal illness or through conflict and war as the technique captures the longevity of the pain experienced.

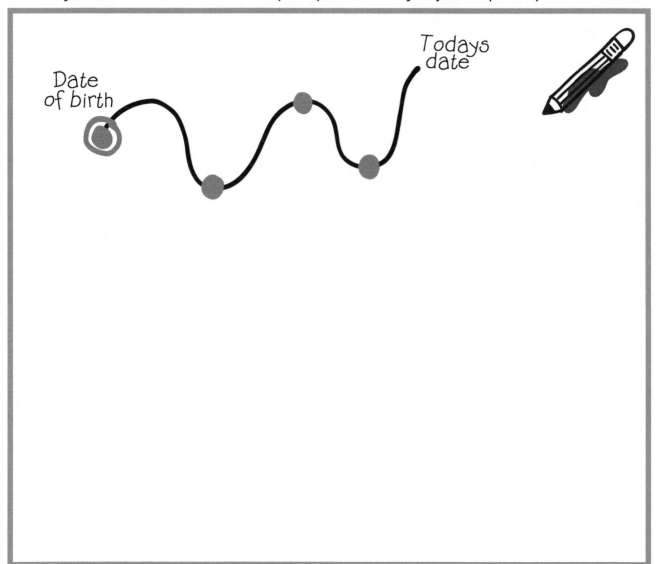

© Copyright TINA RAE 2023

6 HANDOUT/ ACTIVITY SHEET

Understanding
and **Supporting**
Refugee Children
and **Young People**
**A Practical Resource for Teachers,
Parents** and **Carers of Those
Exposed to the Trauma of War**

MY tree of life

Complete your own tree of life.
Make use of the **format below**
and include all the following
information on each different
part of the tree:

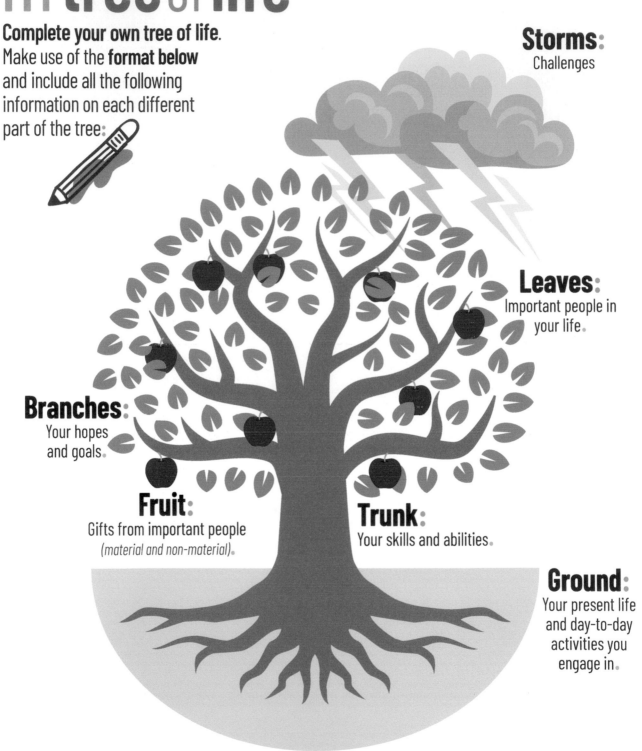

Storms:
Challenges

Leaves:
Important people in
your life.

Branches:
Your hopes
and goals.

Fruit:
Gifts from important people
(material and non-material).

Trunk:
Your skills and abilities.

Ground:
Your present life
and day-to-day
activities you
engage in.

Roots:
Where you come from and
your family.

© Copyright TINA RAE 2023

7 HANDOUT/ ACTIVITY SHEET

Understanding and Supporting Refugee Children and Young People
A Practical Resource for Teachers, Parents and Carers of Those Exposed to the Trauma of War

PAGE **91**

My memory stones

Collect a selection of different stones and pebbles.

These should vary in terms of size, appearance and texture. Then pick out a number of stones to represent different memories you have of the person who has died or has been left behind in the war zone.

You might want to **pick a really shiny stone that represents a time when you made that person proud**, or a **really sparkly stone that reminds you of a special occasion they celebrated**.

Also **select some stones that are maybe more dull, or have sharp edges.** These stones can represent *more painful or difficult memories*.

Then share these memories you have selected with a trusted adult.

You can place the stones in a box to keep them safe but also so you can take them away and possibly share these memories with someone else in the future.

© Copyright TINA RAE 2023

8 HANDOUT/ ACTIVITY SHEET

Understanding and **Supporting Refugee Children** and **Young People**
A Practical Resource for Teachers, Parents and Carers of Those Exposed to the Trauma of War

Recognising feelings
INFORMATION SHEET

Feelings are the **emotions** you **experience** in your **body** and **heart**.

There are many *different feelings* that you may have, and your feelings *may change* from moment to moment. Sometimes you might even feel two or more feelings at the same time. There are no good or bad feelings, but there are positive and negative ways of expressing feelings.

Please write down as many feelings as you can think of below or set a timer for a minute and see how many feelings you can name.

How would you describe these feelings?
Are there colours associated with them?
Can you think of a situation for each experience?

1
2
3
4
5
6
7
8
9
10

11
12
13
14
15
16
17
18
19
20

© Copyright TINA RAE 2023

9 HANDOUT/ ACTIVITY SHEET

Understanding and **Supporting** **Refugee Children** and **Young People**
A Practical Resource for Teachers, Parents and Carers of Those Exposed to the Trauma of War

PAGE **93**

Experiencing feelings in your body

Please colour in the places on your body where you experience each feeling and draw or tell a trusted adult what it feels like.

One way to understand your emotions is by paying attention to your body.

When something stressful happens, **do you get a feeling in the pit of your stomach? Or do your muscles get tight?**

Your body might give you signs to understand your emotions.

Let's look back at the feelings you listed in the Recognising feelings activity. You don't have to do all the feelings you listed but for each feeling you choose, close your eyes or look down and imagine having that feeling right now.

Where do you experience that feeling in your body?

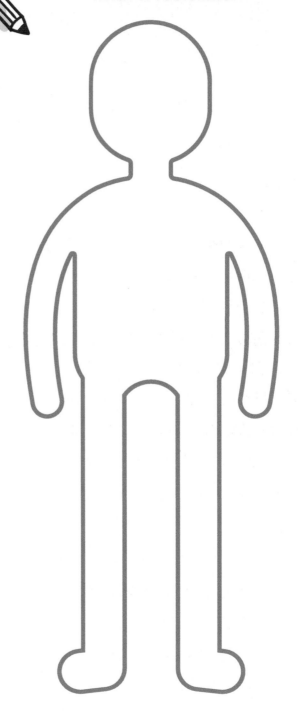

© Copyright TINA RAE 2023

Understanding
and **Supporting**
Refugee Children
and **Young People**
A Practical Resource for Teachers,
Parents and **Carers of Those**
Exposed to the Trauma of War

4 simple strategies for managing anxiety

Ground Your Senses
Find... **5** things you can see
4 things you can hear
3 things you can feel
2 things you can smell or taste
Take **1** deep breath...

When might you use this?

Challenge yourself

Pick something that is challenging enough to occupy your mind, but not so challenging to add to your stress

(e.g. Recite the alphabet backwards or count back from 50 in 3s, count the red things in the room)

When might you use this?

Do something that makes you laugh

It's very difficult to feel anxious and laugh at the same time. Do something that makes **you laugh** *(e.g. watch something funny on YouTube, speak to a friend).*

When might you use this?

Do some exercise

Running or playing sport can burn nervous energy, help you to breath more deeply and distract your mind. The endorphins that will be released will also help you to feel calmer and happier.

When might you use this?

© Copyright TINA RAE 2023

Understanding
and **Supporting**
Refugee Children
and **Young People**
A Practical Resource for Teachers,
Parents and **Carers of Those**
Exposed to the Trauma of War

3 KIND ACTS AND **3** GOOD THINGS DIARY

Sometimes when we are feeling very anxious a simple way of managing this is to reflect on positives and things that we can do for others.

This helps us to think about ourselves in a more positive light to because we are not simply concerned with our own feelings and situations.

Create your own three kind acts and three good things diary.

Every day record three kind things that you will do for others and do them!

At the end of each day record three good things about the day so that you go to bed thinking happy thoughts and not reflecting on all the things that you were worried about.

USE A FORMAT LIKE THIS:

Kind acts
about today:

1

2

3

Good things
about today:

1

2

3

© Copyright TINA RAE 2023

12 HANDOUT/ ACTIVITY SHEET

Understanding
and **Supporting**
Refugee Children
and **Young People**
A Practical Resource for Teachers,
Parents and Carers of Those
Exposed to the Trauma of War

Positive remembering

Remembering past events, situations or people with love and affection and in a positive way is a very important way of maintaining wellbeing and good self-esteem. It is particularly useful to develop the ability to transport yourself to positive past times when times get tough or challenging.

Create your Positive Memories Collage in the format below and include events, people and objects!

MY POSITIVE MEMORIES COLLAGE

© Copyright TINA RAE 2023

13 HANDOUT/ ACTIVITY SHEET

Understanding and **Supporting Refugee Children and Young People**
A Practical Resource for Teachers, Parents and Carers of Those Exposed to the Trauma of War

PAGE 97

3 Mindful Breathing exercises

When you first begin to feel anxious or overwhelmed, it can be helpful to make use of breathing exercises. These are very effective and easy to use without being obvious if you are outside or in a classroom.

Have a go at these simple exercises next time you begin to feel worried or upset and see what a difference they can make.

Use a Breathing Ball

Breathe in for 4 seconds, hold for 4 seconds, *and* breathe out for 4 seconds.
Repeat this 3 times and build it up to 5-10.

5 Finger Breathing

Use your opposite hand's thumb.
As you move slowly up your opposite hand's thumb, **breathe in**. As you move slowly down between fingers, **breathe out**.
Repeat on all five fingers.

Wood Cutter Breaths

Standing normally, take a slow deep breath in and go onto your tippy toes with both hands high above your head. Then breathe out quickly, bringing your head and hands low between your legs as if cutting wood.

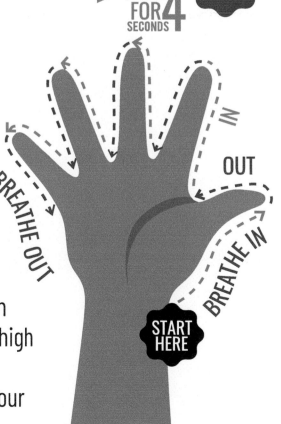

HOLD FOR 4 SECONDS
BREATHE OUT FOR 4 SECONDS
BREATHE IN 4 FOR SECONDS
HOLD FOR 4 SECONDS
START HERE

IN
OUT
BREATHE OUT
BREATHE IN
START HERE

© Copyright TINA RAE 2023

14 HANDOUT/ ACTIVITY SHEET

Understanding and Supporting
Refugee Children and Young People
A Practical Resource for Teachers, Parents and Carers of Those Exposed to the Trauma of War

Progressive Muscle Relaxation

Try out progressive muscle relaxation which is a technique that can help to relieve tension and can help you to sleep at night.

Follow the simple instructions.

1. **Find a space where you can relax** and allow yourself at least 10 minutes for this exercise. Get into a comfortable position, and focus on your breathing, taking deep breaths in through the nose, and out through the mouth.

2. **Starting at your feet**, tense all the muscles from your toes, to the arches of your feet and your ankles, and hold for 10 seconds. Then release and relax for 20 seconds.

3. **Work up your body from your feet** all the way up to your head, isolating areas of the body, tensing, holding and then releasing. Do this with your feet, lower legs, upper legs, bottom, abdomen, chest, hands, arms, shoulders and neck, and finally, your head.

4. **Take time to notice** the difference between the tensed muscles and the soft, relaxed muscles elsewhere in your body.

5. **At the end**, take a moment to focus on the breath and notice how heavy and relaxed your body feels before continuing with your day, or drifting off into a peaceful sleep.

© Copyright TINA RAE 2023

15 HANDOUT/ ACTIVITY SHEET

Understanding and **Supporting** **Refugee Children** and **Young People**
A Practical Resource for Teachers, Parents and Carers of Those Exposed to the Trauma of War

PAGE **99**

Thought troubles

Sometimes we all have thoughts that either aren't completely true and/or are not helpful to us. Some of these thought troubles involve thinking that everything has to be all or nothing.

(*"If one person made fun of me, that means everyone hates me"*).

Other thought troubles focus on the worst possible outcome.

(*"If my Mum goes out, I'm sure something terrible is going to happen to her"*).

You might sometimes get stuck in negative thinking.

(*"Nothing ever works out for me"* or *"I'll never feel OK again"*).

Sometimes even thoughts that are true can cause trouble.

For example, it may be true that you failed a test, but focusing on that failure may not be helpful because it might leave you feeling depressed.

Instead it might be more helpful to think about how you are going to study harder for the next test.

Write about some thought troubles that you've had recently, how you felt, and what you did.

Did you like the way the thoughts made you feel?

How did the situation work out?

Can you imagine it going differently?

If so, how?

Who or what *might help you?*

© Copyright TINA RAE 2023

PAGE 100

16 HANDOUT/ACTIVITY SHEET

Understanding and **Supporting** Refugee Children and **Young People**
A Practical Resource for Teachers, Parents and Carers of Those Exposed to the Trauma of War

Thought Challenging

There are 8 types of negative thinking – Do you need to reflect and challenge yourself?

1	**All or nothing thinking**	This is thinking that is in '**black and white terms**'. These are either the best or worst and there is nothing in between.
2	**Magnifying**	This is exaggerating the importance of what has happened.
3	**Should/must statement**	This is when you set yourself goals that you think you '**have**' to do. These are often too high and unrealistic and can place a lot of pressure on you to reach them.
4	**Magical thinking/ mindreading**	This is when you think you know how someone else is feeling or what they are thinking but don't have much evidence to say why you think this.
5	**Over personalisation**	When you take responsibility for something which was not in your control.
6	**Negative bias**	This is when you find yourself believing that bad things always happen to you.
7	**Labelling**	You attach a label to yourself (or others) and believe this is who you (or they) are.
8	**Catastrophising**	This is when one thing happens and '**snowballs**' to become a series of negative events.

Stop and think!

It is important to remember that our thoughts are not facts, and often our minds give us negative thoughts automatically without considering all of the information. Taking time to do this can help to balance your thinking, thus impacting on the way that you feel and behave.

Test your thought and take the challenge!

MY THOUGHT -

- **What** is the evidence *for* your thought?
- **What** the evidence *against* your thought?
- **What** thinking error *could* you be making? (e.g. catastrophising, black and white thinking, etc.)
- **What** would you say to a friend with that thought?
- **What** would your friend say if they heard your thought?
- **What** is a more positive, energising thought?

© Copyright TINA RAE 2023

Understanding and **Supporting** **Refugee Children** and **Young People** A Practical Resource for Teachers, Parents and Carers of Those Exposed to the Trauma of War

Writing about worries

What is important is to write about how you feel, describe your worries, and then take the time to reflect on them.

DIARY

When we are feeling worried and can't stop our minds from buzzing, it can be helpful to write down the worries in the form of a diary. You don't have to worry about spelling or punctuation. You don't have to worry about making sense of everything.

- **Look back at what you've written and use a highlighter pen to highlight any words that keep coming up again and again. Go back and read through those particular passages.**
- **This can help you to see where you've got some knots in your thinking that might need to be unpicked.**
- **Stop, think *and* reflect. What is really causing this worry?**
- **What keeps the worry going?**
- **What can you do to help yourself?**
- **Who can you go to to talk to to help you unpick this *'Worry Knot'*?**
- **Make up your own 'writing about worries' journal using an exercise book or small hardback book that you can easily buy.**

Make sure that you have someone you can talk to about your worries when you need to.

© Copyright TINA RAE 2023

Understanding
and Supporting
Refugee Children
and Young People
A Practical Resource for Teachers,
Parents and Carers of Those
Exposed to the Trauma of War

Memory BOX

It is important to remember all the good times that we have had in our lives. We can think back, visualise them and even remember the smells, the sights and the tastes of everything about that situation or the individual person who meant so much to us.

Take some time to create your own memory box. Find an appropriate box and decorate it according to your own taste, then collect all the items which hold special memories for you, particularly those that are happy and remind you of good times.

You can then go through this memory box reliving those memories as and when you need to. This helps us to anchor back to good times and gives us hope for the future that we can and will be happy again.

© Copyright TINA RAE 2023

19 HANDOUT/ ACTIVITY SHEET

Understanding and Supporting Refugee Children and Young People
A Practical Resource for Teachers, Parents and Carers of Those Exposed to the Trauma of War

PAGE **103**

MY worries ACTION PLAN

What are the triggers for my **worries?**

How does my body feel when I am **worried?**

What thoughts go through my head when **worried?**

What positive thoughts can I think **instead?**

What helps when I start to feel **worried?**

What can I do to support my wellbeing **every day?**

Who can I talk to at **school?**

Who can I talk to at **home?**

Who can I talk to at **3am?**

Who can I talk to when I am alone?

Apps, **websites** or **phonelines** that help me...

© Copyright TINA RAE 2023

Understanding
and **Supporting**
Refugee Children
and **Young People**
**A Practical Resource for Teachers,
Parents** and **Carers of Those
Exposed to the Trauma of War**

MY
Anxiety
Ladder

Situation

1

2

3

4

5

6

7

8

9

10

You can help yourself to face your fears by using the anxiety ladder.

This involves working out as many gentle steps as possible to build up exposure to the feared thing. **For example**, *if you are afraid of dogs, a ladder may begin with hearing about a dog or looking at a picture of one*

You can draw a ladder with 10 or more steps and then write

down all of the gentle, easy steps you can gradually face in order to conquer the fear.

You can write a step on each rung

Begin with the easiest step on the ladder and build up very, very slowly, noticing and celebrating every step of the way. As you continue over time, you will build up good evidence that it is okay to be with the feared object or situation, and that fears do not have to be there forever.

© Copyright TINA RAE 2023

21 HANDOUT/ACTIVITY SHEET

Understanding and Supporting Refugee Children and Young People
A Practical Resource for Teachers, Parents and Carers of Those Exposed to the Trauma of War

PAGE **105**

MY Calm Space

Visualise a place in which you feel totally at peace.

You can close your eyes if this helps and create the image in your mind.

This may be a place that you been to before or it may be something imaginary such as a beautiful beach, a calming lake, or a peaceful woodland.

Think about the images that you see in front of you, their colours and the noises they make alongside the smells you experience and the things that you can touch too.

THEN USE THIS DRAWING FRAME TO DRAW OUT YOUR CALM PLACE.

Remember to go back there next time you feel worried or unsafe.

© Copyright TINA RAE 2023

Understanding
and **Supporting**
Refugee Children
and **Young People**
A Practical Resource for Teachers,
Parents and Carers of Those
Exposed to the Trauma of War

Good Sleep CHECKLIST

Getting a good night's sleep is essential for being able to effectively regulate our emotions and stay calm. Everyone has had the experience of feeling more irritable, anxious or tearful when tired, so use this checklist to help yourself to have the best chance of having a peaceful rest when you go to bed at night.

Stop, think and reflect!

How many of the following can you tick against in order to make sure that you have a good night sleep?

- ▣ Go to bed at a time that will allow you the opportunity to get at least 9 hours sleep.
- ▣ Avoid any screen time in the hour before bed.
- ▣ Try not to watch television in bed, and you may like to put your mobile away in another room to avoid temptation.
- ▣ Do exercise during the day but avoid any strenuous exercise just before you go to bed.
- ▣ Having a warm bath in the 2 hours before you go to bed can help to cool down the core body temperature to allow you to more easily drift off to sleep.
- ▣ Get the environment right! Ensure your bedroom is darkened, and cool in temperature.
- ▣ Beds should just be for sleeping in. Avoid doing homework in bed.
- ▣ Avoid alcohol and drugs and any stimulant that will make you feel more tired and less rested.
- ▣ Avoid drinking too many fluids during the hour before bed.
- ▣ Use mindfulness, progressive muscle relaxation and meditation to help you to relax.
- ▣ Keep to a consistent sleep routine including at weekends wherever possible.
- ▣ Aim to have some time outdoors in the daylight during the morning to regulate yourself.

© Copyright TINA RAE 2023

23 HANDOUT/ ACTIVITY SHEET

Understanding and Supporting Refugee Children and Young People
A Practical Resource for Teachers, Parents and Carers of Those Exposed to the Trauma of War

PAGE
107

Hopes and dreams heart

- What are your hopes and dreams for the future?
- No matter what happens to us it's important we hold onto these!
- We all need hope and to feel that we have a future that will be something special.
- Draw your hopes and dreams in the heart below.

© Copyright TINA RAE 2023

Understanding
and **Supporting**
Refugee Children
and **Young People**
A Practical Resource for Teachers,
Parents and Carers of Those
Exposed to the Trauma of War

MY Happiness Log

It's not always easy to keep positive and look on the bright side particularly when we are feeling anxious or worried.

However, this is important because even finding the smallest things to be thankful and grateful for on a daily basis can help boost mood.

Use the diary format (*right*) to keep a happiness log.

Record in words and pictures even the smallest things that made you feel happy each day during the week.

At the end of the week reflect on this and notice the difference it makes to your overall mood.

My happiness log.

Monday
_____
_____
_____

Tuesday
_____
_____
_____

Wednesday
_____
_____
_____

Thursday
_____
_____
_____

Friday
_____
_____
_____

Saturday
_____
_____
_____

Sunday
_____
_____
_____

© Copyright TINA RAE 2023

25 HANDOUT/ ACTIVITY SHEET

Understanding and **Supporting** **Refugee Children** and **Young People** A Practical Resource for Teachers, Parents and Carers of Those Exposed to the Trauma of War

PAGE **109**

MY wellbeing AND safetyPLAN

There are five keys to our wellbeing as follows:

1. Connect - this is to be social and to make an effort to connect with someone each day. **Message or meet up with someone who makes you feel good.**

2. Be active - 30 minutes of activity each day is said to keep your **emotional wellbeing protected.**

3. Keep learning - reflect each day on one thing you learned that day. *It may be about any topic. Did you learn a key fact in history? Did you learn about a chemical reaction? Did you learn what is important to a friend? What do you know today that you did not know yesterday?*

4. Give - this keeps happy hormones active in our minds and bodies. **Try it**, think of ways you can give and who to. It may be giving your time to read with a younger sibling, giving help to an older person, or a gift to a friend.

5. Be mindful - Being mindful is about enjoying the time here and now, not wishing you were somewhere else or thinking what is for dinner. **We know that appreciating the senses present in the moment encourages our bodies to work better.**

Think about what you do for each of these. How can you timetable these into your daily routine?

In order to maintain our wellbeing we also have to keep safe. We can do this by identifying our support system.

There are people who care about you and your safety. These are people you can go to if you need help or if you want someone to talk to. This might include family members, friends, teachers, *etc*. Identify your support system by writing the names and/or drawing pictures of all the people who support you and help keep you safe. You can include their phone numbers or contact information, too. You can also write down what kind of support each person can provide or the type of problem you might go to them for.

My safe people are:

1
_____

2
_____

3
_____

4
_____

5
_____

© Copyright TINA RAE 2023

CHAPTER 7

Handouts and resources for **carers** and **professionals**

This chapter **covers**

NUMBER OF PAGES
FOR EACH TOPIC

A. 1 **Understanding trauma information sheet**
B. 1 **Growing stronger from trauma worksheet**
C. 1 **Strategies to manage stress**
D. 1/2/3 **Creating trauma-informed classrooms**
E. 1/2 **Emotionally based school avoidance** (EBSA)
F. 1/2 **Anger management strategies**
G. 1/2 **Top tips for supporting children with grief and loss**
H. 1 **11 coping skills to practise with children**
I. 1 **Top tips for teaching children self-control and regulation**
J. 1 **8 ways a child's anxiety shows up something else**
K. 1 **8 ways to help calm anxiety for adults**
L. 1 **Sleep issues information sheet**
M. 1/2 **Using the FIRE framework to recognise signs of distress**
N. 1 **Managing anxiety** - *common-sense things we can all do*
O. 1/2 **Understanding responses to trauma**
P. 1 **Setting up Calm corners information sheet**
Q. 1/2 **Self-care ideas for adults**
R. 1 **Understanding dysregulation and using the 3R's**
S. 1 **Panic attacks** - *some helpful reminders*
T. 1 **Suicide information sheet**
U. 1 **Positive remembering**
V. 1 **The power of journaling for wellbeing**
W. 1/2 **Supervision and support information sheet**
X. 1 **Useful assessments**
Y. 1 **Helpful websites**

Understanding and Supporting
Refugee Children and Young People:
A Practical Resource for Teachers, Parents and Carers of Those Exposed to the Trauma of War

This chapter presents a range of useful handouts and resources for **carers** and **professionals**.

These can be used in a flexible way with individuals or groups.

The handouts and activity sheets are straightforward with easy-to-follow instructions.

It is therefore possible to make use of them without the need for additional instructions other than those that are provided.

The activities include information on understanding anxiety, trauma, and feelings and how to keep safe emotionally via self care and how to develop develop self-regulation skills and ways of managing worries and make use of tools which ensure post-traumatic growth. There are also useful tools and strategies to manage children and young people with grief and loss, developing coping skills, anger management tools, sleep problems and regulation skills.

Handouts and activities are as follows:

A. UNDERSTANDING TRAUMA INFORMATION SHEET

B. GROWING STRONGER FROM TRAUMA WORKSHEET

C. STRATEGIES TO MANAGE STRESS

D. CREATING TRAUMA-INFORMED CLASSROOMS

E. EMOTIONALLY BASED SCHOOL AVOIDANCE (EBSA)

F. ANGER MANAGEMENT STRATEGIES

G. TOP TIPS FOR SUPPORTING CHILDREN WITH GRIEF AND LOSS

H. 11 COPING SKILLS TO PRACTISE WITH CHILDREN

I. TOP TIPS FOR TEACHING CHILDREN SELF-CONTROL AND REGULATION

J. 8 WAYS A CHILD'S ANXIETY SHOWS UP SOMETHING ELSE

K. 8 WAYS TO HELP CALM ANXIETY FOR ADULTS

L. SLEEP ISSUES INFORMATION SHEET

M. USING THE **FIRE** FRAMEWORK TO RECOGNISE SIGNS OF DISTRESS

N. MANAGING ANXIETY – COMMON-SENSE THINGS WE CAN ALL DO

O. UNDERSTANDING RESPONSES TO TRAUMA

P. SETTING UP CALM CORNERS INFORMATION SHEET

Q. SELF-CARE IDEAS FOR ADULTS

R. UNDERSTANDING SELF REGULATION AND USING THE **3**R'S

S. PANIC ATTACKS: *SOME HELPFUL REMINDERS*

T. SUICIDE INFORMATION SHEET

U. POSITIVE REMEMBERING

V. THE POWER OF JOURNALING FOR WELLBEING

W. SUPERVISION AND SUPPORT INFORMATION SHEET

X. USEFUL ASSESSMENTS

Y. HELPFUL WEBSITES

A
HANDOUT/ ACTIVITY SHEET

Understanding and **Supporting** **Refugee Children** and **Young People**
A Practical Resource for Teachers, Parents and Carers of Those Exposed to the Trauma of War

PAGE
113

Understanding trauma
INFORMATION SHEET

Every child and young person will respond differently to trauma. This means it can be difficult for you to spot the signs, or to see the links between a previous traumatic experience and a child's current feelings and behaviour. Sometimes a child may not be aware of the links themselves.

Some children may show they are struggling immediately after a traumatic experience. But feelings, thoughts and behaviours may also emerge over time. There may be times when things feel intensely difficult, and then they might feel better for a while.

While there is no exhaustive list, **these are some things you may observe** a child doing or experiencing **following a trauma**:

- Having memories, thoughts or flashbacks that seem to come suddenly from nowhere (often called '*intrusive*' thoughts)
- Acting out or having angry or aggressive outbursts
- Finding it difficult to calm down when they are distressed
- Withdrawing from friends, family, school and activities they usually enjoy
- Repeating certain behaviours or seeming agitated
- Avoiding thinking about, talking about or being in situations which are related to a particular experience
- Seeming sensitive or vigilant about anything that could be threatening
- Seeming zoned-out or disconnected from themselves, their feelings and what's going on around them
- Having trouble remembering things
- Not feeling able to sleep or having nightmares
- Using drugs or alcohol differently to how they did before, or starting to for the first time
- Eating significantly more or less
- Self-harming.

These responses are often a young person's way of trying to manage and express difficult feelings. They may feel that some of these behaviours help them to survive or cope, make sense of what's happened, or have a sense of safety and control.

Underneath these kinds of behaviours, **a young person who has experienced trauma may be feeling**:

- ANXIOUS
- ANGRY
- FRIGHTENED
- UNSAFE
- NUMB
- LOW OR DEPRESSED
- ISOLATED
- GUILTY
- ASHAMED
- BAD ABOUT THEMSELVES

TOP TIPS

- Children in care are likely to have experienced trauma but not all children who have adverse experiences will be traumatised. Every child is unique and their responses to the same adversity will differ.
- Trauma can affect brain development. Many traumatised children function at an earlier developmental level than their chronological age suggests.
- Traumatised children may struggle to develop regulatory skills needed for learning and social relationships.

- Some children react powerfully to sensory triggers related to their trauma by becoming hyper-aroused or dissociating. These reactions often occur below the level of conscious awareness.
- *If adults involved with traumatised children are unable to manage their own emotions, this can escalate children's distress.*
- Effective help requires intervention that is congruent with neuroscience, developmentally relevant and relational.
- The key adults in helping children recover from trauma are their carers and teachers. They require relevant support and training to be most helpful to traumatised children.
- *Post-traumatic growth and resilience is possible.* Traumatised children need hope and adults involved with them must believe in a positive future for them.

© Copyright TINA RAE 2023

**Understanding
and Supporting
Refugee Children
and Young People**
A Practical Resource for Teachers,
Parents and Carers of Those
Exposed to the Trauma of War

Growing Stronger from Trauma Worksheet

We all need to try and find the silver linings of a traumatic experience, while appreciating the strengths that we have developed as a result.

Use this framework to explore the strengths that you used to cope with your past trauma, and the new ones you've come out with as a result.

The **goal** of this exercise is to help you cultivate a more balanced, positive perspective on trauma and adversity while recognising ways to deal with future challenges.

Start by listing **five** personal strengths that you already possessed prior to your experience:

1 _____
2 _____
3 _____
4 _____
5 _____

Next, identify those that you believe helped you to cope with the trauma. Taking some time to consider how you've developed, next list any new strengths that you feel you've developed as a result:

New strengths

1 _____
2 _____
3 _____
4 _____
5 _____

Use additional sheets of paper/your journal to reflect on your new strengths; write freely about how you feel about them.

© Copyright TINA RAE 2023

C HANDOUT/ ACTIVITY SHEET

Understanding and **Supporting** **Refugee Children** and **Young People**
A Practical Resource for Teachers, Parents and Carers of Those Exposed to the Trauma of War

PAGE **115**

Strategies to manage stress
The '5' Looks

1. LOOK ABOUT!

- Try to measure the level of stress you are coping with.
- Try to include usual daily hassles and things that you have adapted to recently.
- Remember – not all changes are negative **BUT** they may be a drain on your energy.

2. LOOK TO YOURSELF!

- Try to regularly reflect on your own symptoms – are you getting anxious or irritable?
- Are you trying to do too much or becoming inactive?
- Try to identify any changes that may be due to a build-up of stress.
- Try to **THINK** about the way you think, act and feel.

3. LOOK FORWARDS!

Always try to think about **SOLUTIONS** and particularly focus on whether the solutions you choose will be useful both in the short and long term.

4. LOOK BACK!

- Think about what worked before and learn from the most helpful and useful patterns of behaviour and strategies.
- Try to learn from the less helpful responses – what could you do differently next time?

5. LOOK AFTER YOURSELF!

- Pace yourself and try to do one thing at a time *e.g. eat, rest, see friends* etc. without doing other things at the same time.
- Use **LISTS** to aid memory and prioritise.
- Take breaks when the pressure builds up.
- Use breathing, relaxation and exercise and keep to a healthy diet and lifestyle.
- Give yourself treats and rewards.
- Try to reframe negative self-talk and respect yourself.
- Try to enjoy life and your relationships!

© Copyright TINA RAE 2023

D1 HANDOUT/ACTIVITY SHEET

Understanding
and **Supporting**
Refugee Children
and Young People
A Practical Resource for Teachers,
Parents and **Carers of Those**
Exposed to the Trauma of War

Creating Trauma-Informed Classrooms

This information sheet it is intended to provide you with an overview of what a trauma-informed classroom would look like and key attributes of a trauma-informed approach to supporting children and young people.

We know that having a warm, healthy relationship with an adult can be healing for children who have experienced trauma. These relationships provide safety and grounding. Fostering these types of relationships in the classroom can create safety for all students.

CAPPD

This acronym provides a guideline of trauma-informed relationship building.

Calm **The goal is to create a relaxed, focused state for yourself and your students.** Learning to regulate emotions and return to a relaxed state after being alarmed or triggered helps children function in the neocortex, which is responsible for complex thinking and learning.

Attuned **Be aware of children's non-verbal cues including body language, tone of voice, and emotional state.** These cues indicate how much and what types of activities and learning the child can manage. You must connect with a child on an emotional, sensory level before moving to a cognitive level.

Present **Be in the moment and focus your attention on the child.** All children can tell when people are not truly engaged or paying attention to them.

Predictable **Provide children with routine, structure, and repeated positive experiences.** This will help children to feel safe and allow them to be free to grow and explore.

Don't **let children's emotions escalate your own.** Remain in control of your own emotions and the expression of them. The best way for children to learn to regulate their emotions is by watching us regulate ours.

© Copyright TINA RAE 2023

Understanding and **Supporting** **Refugee Children** and **Young People**
A Practical Resource for Teachers, Parents and Carers of Those Exposed to the Trauma of War

PAGE
117

D2 HANDOUT/ ACTIVITY SHEET

Creating Trauma-Informed Classrooms

Top strategies
Structure and consistency

Providing emotional consistency and clear interpersonal boundaries signals safety for children who have experienced trauma.

- Providing structure & consistency in your own responses will help children regulate as their own internal structure for regulation may not be available.
- Keep regular routines, warn of disruption to routines, and give time and supervision for transitions.
- Provide consistent expectations, limits, and routines.
- Limits are most useful when they are immediate, related, age-appropriate, proportional, and delivered to the child in a calm and respectful voice.
- When setting limits, name the inappropriate behaviours and follow through with consequences.

Give Choices and Control

- Misbehaving is a way for children to have control. Give back control by giving choices.
- "You can finish that work standing up or sitting down".
- "Do you want to wear your coat or carry it to the playground?".

Trauma-informed teaching strategies can build safety in the classroom through consistency, structure, compassion, and understanding. New learning cannot take place if a child does not feel safe. By ensuring safety in the classroom, all students benefit from a safe and compassionate space needed to take emotional and intellectual risks when learning.

Create
Physical Safety

- Be aware of personal space.
- Provide appropriate physical touch when a child seeks it.
- Ask permission before any physical contact.
- Giving unwanted or unasked-for affection can re-traumatise or trigger a child.
- Physical comfort can help calm children and help them learn to regulate their emotions.

and Emotional Safety

- Designate time and space for a child living with trauma to talk about it if they wish so the child knows it's ok to talk about what is happening for them.
- Recognise environmental triggers: weather, anniversaries of loss or trauma.
- Prepare for difficulties; for example, if a child does not like to be alone, provide a buddy to go with them to the cloakroom.
- Support religious beliefs. If trauma is attributed to higher power let the child have their own beliefs, refer to someone of this belief if needed.

Monitor children - *children are very honest*.

Traumatised children are often very sensitive to teasing/bullying and can feel unsafe. Act as a buffer, and let the child know they are being watched out for.

© Copyright TINA RAE 2023

PAGE
118

D3 HANDOUT/
ACTIVITY
SHEET

Understanding
and **Supporting**
Refugee Children
and **Young People**
A Practical Resource for Teachers,
Parents and **Carers of Those**
Exposed to the Trauma of War

Creating Trauma-Informed Classrooms

Structure and Consistency

Triggers may be managed by maintaining classroom structure and consistency as the classroom becomes a more predictable space. Alert children to any changes in the classroom to provide the students time to adjust.

- Check in at the start of each week and term: "What do you remember from last week? What stands out? Why? What would you like to be the same this week? What would you like to be different?"
- Predictable structure. Structure provides a sense of safety and signals to the child he/she is safe. Avoid overly rigid environments; try finding a balance.
- Discuss future activities which will take place in the next lesson, tomorrow, next week, *etc*.
- Establish a routine to create consistency and predictability.
- Do things at the same time and in the same way as often as possible.
- Inform children of any changes – explain how and why things will change.
- Inform students if the room or other elements of their environment is being changed or moved around.
- Stability helps children regain a sense of trust and control in their lives. It also reassures them that an adult is in charge and will help to keep them safe.
- Safety and stability are necessary for children to be able to function from the neocortex.

Monday Mornings, Daily Timetables, and Class Meetings

- Take time to outline the day.
- Use symbols and pictures of clocks for young children.
- Consider holding a brief class meeting – students can be asked to share about their weekend.
- Some teachers ask for "celebrations or challenges" *(not all students will share challenges because they may not feel it is safe to do so).*
- For safety, seat children in a circle so no one has their back to anyone else.
- Review rules and agreements during class meetings to provide safety.
- If you notice a change in a student's effort, take time to connect with that student *(maybe later in the day or in private).*

Provide Visuals

- Display a visual or picture class timetable. You may want to include pictures of students doing the tasks.
- Set up a mini board outlining what students will need for each lesson or subject.
- Position clocks in view in the classroom and refer to them with cues, such as "We are half way through reading, when the big hand is on the 10 we will have our break time." This can encourage students to stay on task as they can visualise progress to an end point.

Transitions

- Provide structured play opportunities during breaks that build on social skills, team work, or sharing.
- Utilise buddy or peer group interventions such as circle of friends to help students manage change with some support.
- Prepare and engage peers to support specific students through transitions periods.

© Copyright TINA RAE 2023

Understanding and **Supporting** **Refugee Children** and **Young People** A Practical Resource for Teachers, Parents and Carers of Those Exposed to the Trauma of War

PAGE **119**

Emotionally Based School Avoidance (EBSA)

Many children at some time in their school career are challenged by anxiety. School phobia (*known to professionals as emotionally based school avoidance*), a complex and extreme form of anxiety about going to school (*but not of the school itself as the name suggests*), can have many causes and can include related anxiety disorders such as agoraphobia and selective mutism.

Symptoms include stomach aches, nausea, fatigue, shaking, a racing heart and frequent trips to the toilet.

Possible triggers include:

1. Being bullied.
2. Starting school for the first time.
3. Moving to a new area and having to start a new school and make new friends or just changing schools.
4. Being off school for a long time through illness or because of a holiday.
5. Bereavement (*of a person or pet*).
6. Feeling threatened by the arrival of a new baby.
7. Having a traumatic experience such as being abused, being raped, having witnessed a tragic event.
8. Problems at home such as a member of the family being very ill.
9. Problems at home such as marital rows, separation and divorce.
10. Violence in the home or any kind of abuse of the child or of another parent.
11. Not having good friends (*or any friends at all*).
12. Being unpopular, being chosen last for teams and feeling a physical failure (*in games and gymnastics*).
13. Feeling an academic failure.
14. Fearing panic attacks when travelling to school or while in school.

Gathering evidence

It is essential to gather further information from the young person, parent and school staff involved with the young person and put into place strategies to support the young person as soon as possible when these behaviours begin to emerge. A quick response can essentially prevent the behaviours from becoming entrenched and result in much better outcomes for the child. **School-based staff should follow a thorough assess, plan, do and review cycle placing the young person at the heart of the planning and any interventions.**

Assess
Gain a full understanding of the various aspects at play (*child, school and family*)

Plan
Based on information gathered, plan for a realistic small reintegration

Do
Ensure resources and support are in place, good communication with school, family and others

Review
Monitor the progress made and adjust the plan for next steps

© Copyright TINA RAE 2023

E2 HANDOUT/ ACTIVITY SHEET

Emotionally Based School Avoidance (EBSA)

Once a difficulty has been identified there should be a prompt investigation into the reasons for the difficulties. In order for any intervention or support plan to be successful it is essential to gain an understanding of the various aspects causing and maintaining the refusing behaviours. Thambirajah et al., (2008) **highlight the main aims of this analysis as follows:**

- **To confirm that the child is displaying school phobia which is emotionally based as opposed to truancy or parentally condoned absence**
- **To assess the extent and severity of** *(a)* **a school absence,** *(b)* **anxiety and** *(c)* **ascertain the types of anxiety**
- **To gather information regarding the various child, family and school factors that may be contributing to or maintaining the behaviours**
- **To synthesise the available information to develop a practical working hypothesis to then inform the planning of an effective intervention for the child.**

A planned return

Once an assessment has been completed then a return-to-school plan should be drawn up in conjunction with parents, school staff and any other agencies involved.

The meeting may take place at school, in the home or another setting within the community to allow the young person to participate.

The young person's views should be included in the planning even if they do not feel that they are able to attend the meeting.

At this stage, depending on the level of anxiety the young person is displaying and the length of time they have been out of school, **the following possibilities should be considered:**

1. **A return to school on a full timetable**
2. **Implementation of a part-time timetable with a gradual return**
3. **Consultation with CAMHS and other agencies which may, if necessary, lead to a referral for out-of-school tuition as part of a reintegration plan.**

A guide published by Anxiety UK looking at anxiety in the context of school suggests that the following issues need to be considered as part of the reintegration process:

- **Where they are most comfortable sitting in class**
- **Which teachers and members of staff they feel most comfortable with**
- **How they find it easiest to enter the room**
- **Who they have to support them**
- **Whether or not they can cope with being asked questions in class**
- **How they get from class to class**
- **Where they feel comfortable in school if they can't get into class.**

They also suggest that use of, and access to, toilets and eating in front of people in the dining hall can be sources of anxiety and therefore will need to be a consideration for some young people.

What is important to remember is that school-based anxiety takes time to overcome.

It is vital that school-based staff understand anxiety and how it manifests itself in the child's behaviours both emotionally and socially. It is also essential that everyone in the school community understands the need to adopt a nurturing, step-by-step approach to reintegrating any child or young person who has emotionally based school avoidance.

The key strategy overall is to provide the emotional support, never to dismiss the child's genuine fears or concerns, and always to take a step-by-step approach. For example, if a child is petrified of the water then there is no way an adult would ever consider simply throwing them in at the deep end of the swimming pool. They would not swim, they would simply drown. This is no different for a child with school-based anxiety of this nature, and this needs to be the key message provided to all staff in the learning community if they are to truly meet the needs of these children and young people.

© Copyright TINA RAE 2023

F1
HANDOUT/ ACTIVITY SHEET

Understanding
and **Supporting**
Refugee Children
and **Young People**
A Practical Resource for Teachers,
Parents and **Carers of Those**
Exposed to the Trauma of War

PAGE
121

ANGER
Management
Strategies

Children who are experiencing trauma may often present as stressed and angry. It is important to provide them with a range of key tools and strategies that they can make use of in order to manage this effectively, particularly in the school context. However, it is also important to highlight the fact that trauma-related behaviours of this kind should not be punished.

The most important thing is to support the child to regulate by co-regulating with them and giving them a range of key tools and strategies which you model for them and with them.

The most useful and commonly used strategies the young people have evaluated are as follows:

The **traffic light system**

This presents young people with a means of identifying, analysing and subsequently de-escalating strong feelings. **It is a clear visual image of how strong feelings can be managed as follows:**

The red light indicates the stop and think stage in which the pupils identify the problem - What is the problem? How do I feel?

The amber light represents the wait and plan stage - What should I do? Who can help me? What are the consequences?

The green light represents the go stage - try your plan, go for it, reflect, evaluate.

Young people can make use of this traffic light system on a regular basis and evaluate how useful or otherwise it is by referring to their anger log or strong feelings diary. The traffic light strategy can be used as a visual reminder in the form of a book mark and presented in poster form in a range of contexts around the school.

Change your thinking

Once students know what their triggers are they can then begin to change how they think about them by creating a new script. It is useful to present opportunities for triggers to be identified and for young people to then identify what they think and do as a result of these triggers. In true solution-focused fashion they can then proceed to think and articulate what they could do differently, how they could think differently, how they could respond differently in the future.

Developing a script

Students can also develop their own personal calming down script in order to diffuse a situation when they find themselves becoming angry. This can be written down onto a small card and kept somewhere safe.

Using 'I' messages

Young people can formulate an 'I' message which can replace negative responses or statements. For example, if someone is attempting to pick a fight with them or if someone is doing something that is beginning to make them angry they can

© Copyright TINA RAE 2023

F2 HANDOUT/ ACTIVITY SHEET

Understanding and Supporting Refugee Children and Young People
A Practical Resource for Teachers, Parents and Carers of Those Exposed to the Trauma of War

ANGER Management Strategies

rehearse an 'I' statement such as *"I would like you to stop that now because you are making me feel angry"* or *"I don't like what you are doing please stop it"* etc.

Using exercise

Running out your anger or engaging in some form of exercise is particularly helpful as it produces the feel-good chemical endorphins alongside having a further positive pay-off in terms of keeping you fit and reasonably well.

Using the tension scale

Pupils can imagine a tension scale from 0-10 *(10 being the most upset or angry that they could feel and 0 being the state when physiologically they are back to normal)*. They can then proceed through a series of steps: 1) **I am upset because** 2) **I am at point...on the scale** 3) **to get down to point...I need to...** 4) **to get down to point** 0 **I need to...** 5) **when I am on** 0 **I will feel...**

Using a relaxation script

Students can be provided with a relaxation script which they can practise on a regular basis. Tensing and releasing muscles in each part of their body in turn. This can either be read aloud to them or they can commit the script to memory. This can be something they use prior to entering a more stressful situation or subsequent to experiencing a real pressure on their ability to cope and manage their behaviours effectively.

Use of distraction

Adults in a situation can often help a student by distracting them to another activity if they can see that they are becoming angry or stressed by a situation or event.

Students can also make use of distraction for themselves, recognising the trigger to anger and immediately distracting themselves from the situation by engaging in a more positive activity.

Use of relocation or time in a safe space

Very often when things get really stressful students may wish to take time out. Individuals can be issued with time out cards or some other means of indicating to the member of staff that they need to take some time to themselves in order to calm down.

Use of anger spoilers

Students can make use of a range of anger spoilers such as counting to 10 or 100 or traffic lights as detailed above *etc.*

However, with all the above strategies it is particularly important that young people are given the opportunity to actually practise them and review them on a weekly basis; this is the whole purpose of any anger management intervention. It is not simply to present students with a list of tools and ideas but to provide them with opportunities to practise them, try them out and evaluate them. *What works for me? Why does it work? What do I need to do differently in that situation next time?* The key to this particular approach is to try the strategies and then reflect continuously as to why they did or didn't work. It is also vital that both staff and students remain solution focused. If it doesn't work have another go, try again, try something different and keep trying until you find what works for you.

© Copyright TINA RAE 2023

G1

HANDOUT/ ACTIVITY SHEET

Understanding and Supporting Refugee Children and Young People
A Practical Resource for Teachers, Parents and Carers of Those Exposed to the Trauma of War

PAGE **123**

TOP TIPS

For supporting children with grief and loss

The most effective strategy for supporting a child or young person who is experiencing a bereavement is to be available for them so they can talk about what is happening. It might be that they wish to talk about their feelings in the '*here and now*', or they might want to discuss concerns they have about the past or future. Alternatively, they might want to share memories of the person who has died but feel they cannot speak with other family members as it might cause upset.

These are the key things to remember when supporting a child or young person to talk about grief and loss.

Tell the truth

It is important to be open and honest with the child so that they can gain as clear an understanding of the situation as possible. This is not always easy, particularly in more challenging situations, such as a murder or suicide. It might be that the police are still investigating the situation, in which case it is important to provide all the facts that are available to you, whilst remaining objective and not exposing the child to unnecessary or upsetting details.

For example, it might be that you are able to confirm for the child that the person has died, but then explain that you are waiting for the police to tell you more information and that, as soon as that happens, you will let the child know.

Avoid using metaphors

Use words such as '*died*' and '*dead*' rather than '*gone to a better place*' or '*is no longer with us*'. This can be very confusing for a child and they might believe that, ultimately, that person will come back at some point. This is particularly true for younger children who

© Copyright TINA RAE 2023

G2 HANDOUT/ ACTIVITY SHEET

Understanding and **Supporting** **Refugee Children** and **Young People**
A Practical Resource for Teachers, Parents and Carers of Those Exposed to the Trauma of War

TOP TIPS

For **supporting children** with **grief** and **loss**

have not yet established that death is a permanent and irreversible state.

Avoid telling the child not to worry or be sad

Adults naturally wish to reassure children and remove any pain or suffering. However, it is important to recognise that there are a range of intense emotions that are associated with the grieving process and that these all serve to support the child or young person through the experience. It is normal to feel sad, scared, angry or guilty following a loss and you should support the child by acknowledging and normalising these emotions, rather than attempting to dismiss them.

It's OK to cry

Crying is something which has an amount of social stigma attached to it. This is particularly the case for older students and male students. As with acknowledging and normalising the emotions being displayed by the child or young person, you should also acknowledge and normalise crying. To this extent, it is OK for you to cry too. Providing support for the child does not mean that you have to be '*strong*' and show no emotion. Grief is something which effects everybody and can generate strong emotional reactions in people. It is perfectly fine for you to express these emotions alongside the child. However, it is also important that you are aware of the impact that this is having on you and if you feel that you are not the best person to support a child, due to your own personal circumstances, it is important that you put yourself first and explicitly acknowledge this with your line manager.

Provide reassurance

As the child begins to gain an understanding of what has happened, they are likely to feel unsure or unsafe. "*If this has happened to Mummy, what's to stop it happening to Daddy?*" They will therefore require lots of reassurance. This should take the form of reassuring the child that their reaction to the situation is normal (*as mentioned above*).

They should also be reassured that they did not cause the incident and that other people in their lives are safe. This is particularly true for children who are at the '*magical thinking*' stage of development. Depending on the relationship that the child or young person had with the person who had died, they might require additional support in processing feelings such as guilt, for example, if they had previously told that person that they wished they were dead.

Prepare for a variety of emotions

Children can react in many different ways to a death. Depending on their understanding of death, they may appear unaffected. Alternatively, they might '*puddle jump*', in which case it is really important that when you prepare to talk about death with a chid, you are also prepared for a variety of emotions to come from them and that you are able to interpret these emotions as the child coping with processing the information they are receiving, rather than a callous or unemotional response to an upsetting situation.

Repetition

It might take a number of discussions before the child is able to process and understand what is being said. An element of that might be shock, for example if someone has died unexpectedly. However, this can also be related to the child's age and stage of development with regard to understanding death and so you might find you are having the same conversation with them on a number of occasions as they attempt to make sense of what is going on around them.

© Copyright TINA RAE 2023

H HANDOUT/ ACTIVITY SHEET

Understanding and **Supporting** **Refugee Children** and **Young People**
A Practical Resource for Teachers, Parents and Carers of Those Exposed to the Trauma of War

PAGE
125

11 coping skills to practise with children

Each week **spend some time with your child** to talk about their thoughts and feelings

1. **Try and focus on the here and now.** Stay in the present moment.

2. **Engage in some deep breathing** for a couple of minutes.

3. **When your child experiences negative thoughts** help them identify thinking errors.

4. **Engage in some self-care.** Do things that provide you with rest and recovery.

5. **Engage in some worry time** and learn how to postpone worries.

6. **Encourage your child** to openly talk about their thoughts and feelings.

7. **Find a moment to get active together** and do some exercise.

8. **Find an activity you can both do mindfully.** Use all your senses.

9. **Identify some of your child's strengths** and how they can use them in the next week.

10. **With your child write down 3 good things** they have achieved in the day.

11. **Choose an activity with your child** and slow everything down. Breathe slower and move slower.

© Copyright TINA RAE 2023

Understanding
and **Supporting**
Refugee Children
and **Young People**
**A Practical Resource for Teachers,
Parents and Carers of Those
Exposed to the Trauma of War**

TOP TIPS

For teaching children self-control and regulation

1. **Get down on their level.** Standing over the child or young person can make them feel overwhelmed; kneeling down creates safety.

2. **Give Empathy.** Feeling heard and understood is a core need that we all have. When we take the time to empathise, children feel understood, which in turn helps them recognise and regulate their emotions.

3. **Match their emotional tone.** Get to a place where you can understand their emotion and match that emotion with your tone of voice. This creates emotional resonance, helping them to feel heard and understood. Mirror for them what you see.

4. **Give them time.** Remain open and loving to their perspective and experience. Slow down and respect them in the moment. Reject the idea that their emotions can be changed for our own convenience.

5. **Let them play.** All children and young people need unstructured time. They should have at least 2.5 to 3 hours a day to make independent choices and to be in charge of their own experiences. Remember we learn through playing.

© Copyright TINA RAE 2023

J HANDOUT/ ACTIVITY SHEET

Understanding and **Supporting** **Refugee Children** and **Young People**
A Practical Resource for Teachers, Parents and Carers of Those Exposed to the Trauma of War

PAGE **127**

8 ways a Child's anxiety shows up as something else

1. **Anger** – the perception of danger, stress or opposition is enough to trigger the fight or flight responses, leaving your child angry and without a way to communicate why.

2. **Difficulty Sleeping** – in children, having difficulty falling asleep or staying asleep is one of the hallmark characteristics of anxiety.

3. **Defiance** – unable to communicate what is really going on, it is easy to interpret the child's defiance as a lack of discipline instead of an attempt to control a situation where they feel anxious or helpless.

4. **Chandeliering** – chandeliering is when a seemingly calm person suddenly flies off the handle for no reason. They have pushed hurt and anxiety so deep for so long that a seemingly innocent comment or event suddenly sends them straight through the chandelier.

5. **Lack of Focus** – children with anxiety are often so caught up in their own thoughts that they do not pay attention to what is going on around them.

6. **Avoidance** – children who are trying to avoid a particular person, place or task often end up experiencing more of whatever it is they are avoiding.

7. **Negativity** – people with anxiety tend to experience negative thoughts at a much greater intensity than positive ones.

8. **Over-planning** – over-planning and defiance go hand in hand in their root cause, where anxiety can cause some children to try to take back control through defiant behaviour, it can cause others to over-plan for situations where planning is minimal or unnecessary.

© Copyright TINA RAE 2023

K HANDOUT/ ACTIVITY SHEET

Understanding and **Supporting** Refugee **Children** and **Young People**
A Practical Resource for Teachers, Parents and Carers of Those Exposed to the Trauma of War

8 ways to help calm anxiety for adults

If you find anxiety is something you struggle with frequently then **check your self-care routines**.

Make sure you get time to do things you enjoy, see others regularly, and have a diet that is rich in a range of nutrients but doesn't have too much alcohol, caffeine or sugar. Ensure that you get some regular physical activity and pay attention to your sleep routine.

1. CONTROL YOUR BREATHING

Try breathing in slowly then out slowly to a count of about 6. As you become calmer you may be able to slow down your breathing even more.

2. STOP TIME TRAVELLING

Anxiety often comes from worrying about things in the future or fretting about things in the past. Try to stay as *'present'* as possible. Mindfulness or meditation can help or concentrate on what you need to do now.

3. REFRAME THOUGHTS

Remind yourself that you have managed to do this before or that you are prepared, or you have the skills you need. Look for the truth of the situation. Talk to yourself as if you were talking to a friend, with kindness.

4. DO SOMETHING

Any activity can help. Make a drink or have a shower, eating and drinking can be soothing.

5. CONNECT WITH SOMEONE

Talking can help a lot, in person is particularly helpful but if that's not possible then by phone or even a **WhatsApp** or text message.

6. DISTRACT YOURSELF

Reading can be calming or even watching short videos especially funny ones, laughter can release feel-good hormones.

7. WRITE IT DOWN

Some people find writing down their worries is a big help. Others go further and write them down and put them away somewhere or even bin them.

8. AFFIRMATIONS

Arm yourself with some positive affirmations you can draw on when you feel anxious. You can start by simply reminding yourself that anxious feelings will pass, but you may want to develop some others linked to what causes anxiety, things like you can be confident, you can do this task *etc.*

© Copyright TINA RAE 2023

L HANDOUT/ ACTIVITY SHEET

Understanding and **Supporting** Refugee Children and **Young People**
A Practical Resource for Teachers, Parents and Carers of Those Exposed to the Trauma of War

PAGE
129

Sleep issues
INFORMATION SHEET

Many children and young people who have experienced trauma will have difficulties in sleeping. Some children will find that the major cause for worry is the fear that they will not be able to sleep. This leads them to begin worrying about sleep many hours before the actual bedtime.

Others may wake up in the middle of the night and start worrying that they won't be able to fall back to sleep again or they may fear experiencing intrusive nightmares.

The following are some simple techniques which may be useful:

1. **Take time to talk to the child at bedtime.** *Set limits around this time but ensure that it includes problem-solving any worries that they may have and then having some problem-free talk for older children, focusing on three good things, or reading a bedside story to younger children.*

2. **Encourage your child to self-regulate before bedtime.** *Make sure that the lights are dimmed and that they have access to a reading book, music tape with a clip-on LED reading light if necessary. Prompt them to make use of any mindfulness strategies or relaxation scripts if this helps.*

3. **Make it a rule of no screens before bed.** *All digital devices need to be removed an hour before bed as blue light emitted from screens can inhibit the body's natural melatonin release.*

4. **Help the child to trick the body into a natural melatonin release by keeping the lights dim and blocking natural light before bedtime.** *We know that melatonin can help children to sleep.*

5. **Teach your child to give their worries away.** *There is a lovely tradition in Guatemala where the adults teach children to give their worries to little colourful dolls or trouble dolls. Children can also give their worries away to another inanimate object or simply write them down and post them into a Worry Box that they can come back to the next day when there is time to go through the worries with you or another trusted adult.*

6. **Keep to routines and make them visual for younger children,** process of bath time, brushing hair, story *etc.*

7. **Use storytime therapeutically.** *Reading something positive about a lovely imaginary world to a child before bedtime can help them to forget their worries and fears.*

8. **Always remove any stimulants** *and ensure no access to high-energy drinks which contain caffeine.*

9. **Regulate any fluid intake before bedtime** *reducing it at least two hours prior to a child going to sleep.*

10. **If the difficulties persist, it is essential to make a referral to the GP or the school nurse** *who can provide additional and more specialist advice and support.*

© Copyright TINA RAE 2023

M1 HANDOUT/ ACTIVITY SHEET

Understanding and **Supporting** Refugee Children and **Young People**
A Practical Resource for Teachers, Parents and Carers of Those Exposed to the Trauma of War

Using the FIRES FRAMEWORK to recognise signs of distress

The following framework is intended for **school-based staff** to support them in the process of identifying children and young people who may be showing signs of mental distress, and consequently you need additional support or intervention.

Fast response

Act quickly when you notice possible signs of mental distress

- Don't ignore it but take action as soon as possible when you can see or hear that a child is having difficulty.
- If possible, speak first to the mental health lead or safeguarding lead and work together to create an appropriate plan.
- Prepare yourself emotionally for the conversation and make sure that you have the information you need in order to be able to respond effectively.
- Make sure that you have appropriate time and space for the conversation with the young person.
- Get down to their level.
- Consider whether you need to make use of eye contact or whether this might increase the child's level of anxiety and prevent a more authentic dialogue.
- Let them know that you're there to talk to them if they'd like to talk to you, but do not push them to open up if they're not ready to do so.
- Make sure that you establish the expectations around confidentiality.
- Remember that it is always best to raise the issue and be wrong than not raise it and be right.

© Copyright TINA RAE 2023

M2 HANDOUT/ ACTIVITY SHEET

Understanding and Supporting Refugee Children and Young People
A Practical Resource for Teachers, Parents and Carers of Those Exposed to the Trauma of War

PAGE
131

Using the FIRES FRAMEWORK

Identify needs and risks

Assess the situation for immediate needs and full risk of harm

- Ask yourself if there are any immediate risks – is a young person at risk to themselves or others at this current time?
- Is there a risk that the young person may be feeling suicidal?
- Is there any way in which the child or young person could harm themselves?
- Could there be a medical emergency for example, cuts, overdose, asthma attack *etc.*?
- Are alcohol or drugs present?
- Does the child or young person need space or do they need closeness?
- Who would be the best person to help in this particular situation?
- Is this environment right for them at this point in time? Can they be moved?

Reassure

Stay calm, unshockable and provide reassurance

- Reassure them that you are there to help and get the support that they need.
- Normalise their feelings but don't belittle their feelings.
- Be sure to take what they are saying seriously.
- Be unshockable and non-judgemental.

Empathise and listen

Listen non-judgementally, validate, accept and empathise

- Make sure you understand the definition of empathy and how to express this.
- Make use of open questions in order to encourage them to communicate and talk to you.
- Offer empathy and understanding rather than solutions.
- Always be patient, friendly and give your full attention to the child or young person.

Signpost and support

Offer support strategies, pass on information, and refer for professional support

- Check with the child whether there is anyone else that they have talked to or could talk to.
- Try to establish protective factors.
- Signpost to other sources of information or support.
- Be clear what you will do with the information that they have told you and who it will be shared with.

© Copyright TINA RAE 2023

PAGE
132

Understanding
and **Supporting**
Refugee Children
and **Young People**
A Practical Resource for Teachers,
Parents and Carers of Those
Exposed to the Trauma of War

Managing Anxiety –
Common-sense things we can all do

There are many common-sense ways in which we can all assist children and young people to manage anxiety more effectively:

● **Support them to challenge underlying beliefs and thoughts**, - Negative and irrational beliefs and thoughts, such as *'If I don't look perfect, no one will like me'*, or *'I can't cope with difficult or scary situations'*, are significant factors in generating anxiety. Model and communicate effective ways to question and challenge anxiety-provoking thoughts and beliefs.

● **Support them to accept uncertainty** - Uncertainty is one thing that people worry about a lot because of the potential for negative outcomes. As it is impossible to eliminate uncertainty, you can assist children and young people to be more accepting of uncertainty and ambiguity.

● **Be a role model** - If you can manage your own anxiety, young people will see that it can be managed and incorporate your strategies into their own behaviours. Teaching parents to manage their own anxiety has been shown to be helpful in reducing their children's anxiety.

● **Be patient** - Sometimes the behaviours of anxious children and teens may seem unreasonable to others. It is important to remember that an anxious young person who cries or avoids situations is, in fact, responding instinctively to a perceived threat. Changing avoidant behaviours takes time and persistence.

● **Balance reassurance with new ideas** - When a child comes to you with something they are worried about, listen and understand what is happening. Explore with them what they could do to manage their fears.

● **Show children and young people some simple relaxation techniques** - Deep breathing, progressive muscle relaxation and meditation can be helpful as a way of learning how to better manage physical anxiety symptoms. Generally, these techniques are only effective if practised consistently over several weeks.

● **Encourage plenty of physical exercise and appropriate sleep** - When people are well-rested and relaxed, they will be in a better mental state to handle fears or worries.

● **Moderate the consumption of caffeine and high-sugar products** - Caffeine products including cola and energy drinks increase levels of anxiety as they cause energy levels to spike and then crash. This leaves a person feeling drained and less able to deal with negative thoughts.

● **Make time for things that the child enjoys and finds relaxing** - These could be simple things like playing or listening to music, reading books or going for walks.

● **Help them to face the things or situations they fear** - Learning to face their fears and reduce avoidance of feared objects and situations is one of the most challenging parts of overcoming anxiety. Facing fears usually works best if it is undertaken gradually, a step at a time.

● **Encourage help-seeking when needed** - Make sure that children and young people know there are people who can help if they find that they can't handle a problem on their own. Knowing that they can call on others for support if needed will make them feel less anxious about what might happen in the future.

© Copyright TINA RAE 2023

01 HANDOUT/ ACTIVITY SHEET

Understanding and **Supporting** **Refugee Children** and **Young People**
A Practical Resource for Teachers, Parents and Carers of Those Exposed to the Trauma of War

PAGE
133

Understanding responses to trauma

There are many common-sense ways in which we can all assist children and young people to manage anxiety more effectively:

Key responses

FIGHT

The fight trauma response involves a release of hormones (*primarily cortisol and adrenaline*) in the body that trigger a reaction to stay and ward off or "***fight***" the apparent threat. The sympathetic nervous system is responsible for the reactions that occur within the body during this stress response.

A healthy example of a fight stress response is fighting off a wild animal attack. This response is appropriate for the threat level, and in this scenario, a fight trauma response can better increase your odds of survival. While a wild animal attack isn't a common threat nowadays, most of us can relate to the experience of being verbally bullied by someone else. When someone speaks to us demeaningly, and we stand up for ourselves and communicate our boundaries, that's a healthy fight response. However, if we decide to punch someone in the face instead, that response is disproportionate to the initial threat.

FLIGHT

The flight trauma response involves a release of stress hormones that signal us to flee from the danger or threat. Instead of staying in a dangerous situation, this response causes us to literally or metaphorically run.

One example of this response is in a robbery situation: *If an armed robber enters your home and you have no defence, your survival instinct may force you to get away from the perceived threat as fast as you can. The flight response occurs through the sympathetic nervous system — it activates the hypothalamus in the brain, which communicates with the rest of the body so that you have the energy to fight or flee.*

FREEZE

The freeze response leaves us temporarily paralysed by fear and unable to move. In this response, rather than fighting off the danger or running away from it, we do nothing; the perceived threat causes a hypotonic or immobile reaction. Someone in a freeze response may experience numbness or a sense of dread.

A good example of a freeze response is when someone experiences "***stage fright***" or freezes in front of a large audience. They may forget their lines or "***freeze***" and not be able to perform due to fear.

FAWN

The fawn response involves complying after you've tried fight, flight, or freeze several times without success. This response to a threat is common for people who have experienced abuse, especially those with narcissistic caregivers.

The fawn response may show up as people-pleasing. You may use compliance and helpfulness to avoid abuse; you disregard your happiness and wellbeing no matter how poorly someone treats you. This trauma response is often used to diffuse conflict and return to a feeling of safety.

FLOP

In a flop trauma response, we become entirely physically or mentally unresponsive and may even faint. Fainting in response to being paralysed by fear is caused when someone gets so overwhelmed by the stress that they physically collapse.

© Copyright TINA RAE 2023

Understanding and **Supporting** Refugee Children and **Young People**
A Practical Resource for Teachers, Parents and Carers of Those Exposed to the Trauma of War

Understanding responses to trauma

THE ROLE OF TRAUMA RESPONSES

All animals *(including humans)* have built-in survival systems. The brain stem oversees these survival systems and chooses a survival response automatically in a split second. We do not have time to consciously decide what to do in a threatening situation — it would take too long and compromise our survival.

In hindsight, people are often confused about why they acted a certain way during a traumatic incident. However, it was probably the only option, given the information the brain received at that particular time. It takes some mastery over ourselves and our emotions to elicit a proper response to triggering situations.

STUCK IN A TRAUMA RESPONSE

Whether you spring into **fight, flight, freeze, flop,** *or* **even fawn,** your survival mechanism is to avoid the danger and return to a sense of control. The stress response can trigger instantaneously, but how soon your body comes back to normal varies from person to person. *On average, it takes 20 to 30 minutes for your physiology to return to normal and for your breathing to slow down.*

However, some people can become stuck in a trauma response. When individuals do not work through their past traumas through various means including self-help groups, meditation, breathing practices, or other tools, they can often get stuck in a rut and revert to unhealthy coping strategies.

Maladaptive coping behaviours, such as alcohol and drug abuse, are sadly common in trauma survivors.

HEALTHY COPING MECHANISMS AND TRAUMA RESOLUTION

Trauma responses occur for several reasons and are often due to unresolved incidents from the past. Our natural reaction is to make a quick decision on how to deal with the situation, and first and foremost, remove ourselves from harm's way. Fortunately, people can learn techniques to counter the stress response.

Methods to calm the stress response may include:

- **YOGA**
- **DEEP BREATHING**
- **VISUALISATION**
- **PRAYER**
- **TAI CHI**
- **PHYSICAL ACTIVITY**
- **SOCIAL SUPPORT**

Managing our trauma is critical to overall health. If your stress levels affect your quality of life, you may need help or tools to reduce the potential for health risks.

When individuals do become stuck it is important that they seek the appropriate professional help from a trauma specialist therapist or counsellor. There is always hope and the possibility of post-trauma growth - even for those who seem particularly entrenched in their behaviours. The important thing to remember is the process of feeling does take time, so patience is always needed.

© Copyright TINA RAE 2023

P HANDOUT/ **P** ACTIVITY SHEET

Understanding and **Supporting** **Refugee Children** and **Young People**
A Practical Resource for Teachers, Parents and Carers of Those Exposed to the Trauma of War

PAGE 135

Setting up Calm corners

INFORMATION SHEET

Creating your Calm corner/room/space in which children and young people can learn how to safely regulate and develop tools and strategies so that they can remain in their window of tolerance.

The Calm corner needs to be a special place of safety where children and young people can give themselves greater opportunities to be resilient and stay calm and focused. Developing their self-awareness and with this, greater levels of adaptability, flexibility and independence are the key objectives of such a space.

5 Keys to setting up the Calm corner space

Key 1 Location

It is important to carefully consider where you will set up your calm down corner. *For example*, you may choose a space in the back of the room, so students using it do not feel self-conscious. The best option of course is to have a dedicated room, but this is a luxury for many in today's current climate. **Ask yourself:**

- Does the space have enough room for a chair/small sofa/bean bag and possibly a small table?
- Does the space seem semi-private?
- Can children easily access the space?

Key 2 Furniture

Furniture is another key factor in creating your calm down corner. The size of the space will determine what you can include. At a minimum, you will need an adequate seating area which includes a *chair/bean bag/small sofa. A small desk or table will also be useful for any self-reflection/recording activities as will a listening booth for access to music tapes/relaxation tapes/online calm down resources*

Key 3 Meaningful visuals

You will need to provide children with visual displays and resources to help them self-regulate and manage their emotions. **For example.**

- A poster with breathing techniques
- A poster asking students to rate their "*emotional temperature*"
- A list of things they could do in the Calm corner
- A resource with strategies for problems solving in a stepped way
- A resource with strategies for using key tools from Mindfulness such as visualisation of my calming place/grounding of my feet to the floor.

Key 4 Calm down tools

A calm down corner is not complete without the physical/tactile tools children can use to help themselves regulate their emotions and return to their window of tolerance. **These might include the following:**

- Glitter jar
- Expandable ball
- Puffer squeeze ball
- Kinetic sand
- Sensory stixx

Key 5 Teach children about the calm down corner

All the children and young people will need to be taught about the calm down corner and why it is such a helpful and essential intervention for our wellbeing. *Why do we need this? What does it help us to do? What are the resources in the corner and how do we use them? When and why?* Spending some time as a whole class to reinforce the purpose and practicalities is obviously an essential.

© Copyright TINA RAE 2023

Q1 HANDOUT/ ACTIVITY SHEET

Understanding and **Supporting** Refugee Children and **Young People**
A Practical Resource for Teachers, Parents and Carers of Those Exposed to the Trauma of War

Self-care ideas FOR ADULTS

We know that it is important that those who nurture traumatised children and young people take care of themselves first.

We also know that self-care can help to minimise the effects of burnout, including depersonalisation, emotional exhaustion, and stress levels.

Here are some very simple ideas for you to consider:

1. **Support system.** Having a support system provides you the opportunity to ask for help, as you need it.

2. **Learn to process feelings.** Master the skill of processing your emotions in a healthy way.

3. **Learn to say no!** Believe in it, practise it, and use it to avoid overwhelm and overextending yourself that leads to burnout and resentment.

4. **Create, believe in, and enforce your own boundaries.** Your boundaries protect you from harm, just as the borders are there to protect countries.

5. **Proper sleep.** Good sleep is imperative for physical and mental health and wellbeing. It provides the body with the rest it needs to keep you well, and helps you perform at your best in all that you have to do on a daily basis.

6. **Eat a healthy diet.** Good food nourishes the body and brain, keeps your weight at a healthy level, and provides you with ample energy.

7. **Practise mindfulness.** Mindfulness is a practice that makes you focus on the present moment and really pay attention to what is going on, including smells, sounds, feelings, actions, and everything else. This practice offers numerous benefits, with one of the best ones being that it keeps you in the present moment and prevents senseless worry about the future or nagging thoughts of the past.

8. **Create a morning routine with meditation, prayer, visualisations, an uplifting podcast, anything that works for you.** Morning rituals help get you centred for the day ahead.

9. **Turn off all noise, including phone, social media alerts, and just sit in silence.** You can do this easy self-care practice during any one of your days.

10. **Practise gratitude.** Gratitude is one of those things that eludes many, as we get caught up in the spiral of daily stress and responsibilities and begin to resent all that we have to do. Being grateful for all we have, even with the frustrations involved helps keep you centred and more calm.

© Copyright TINA RAE 2023

Q2 HANDOUT/ACTIVITY SHEET

Understanding and **Supporting** **Refugee Children** and **Young People**
A Practical Resource for Teachers, Parents and Carers of Those Exposed to the Trauma of War

PAGE **137**

11. **Move away from negative and/or unhealthy people**. People who do not serve a positive purpose in your life only drag you down.

12. **Practise deep breathing several times each day**.

13. **Meditate**. This practice only takes minutes, and can be done anywhere. There are many smartphone apps with guided meditations to help you stop and take care of yourself throughout your day. It helps keep you centred, focused, and relaxed.

14. **Exercise**. All exercise releases feel-good chemicals in the brain, reduces stress, detoxifies the body and greatly improves moovpful.

15. **Practise positivity**. Positive thinking is miraculously healing, and optimists live longer and handle stress much better than pessimists do. Always look for the silver linings in any situation, especially the bad ones. *Stay hopeful*.

16. **Create calming surroundings**. Look around your home, your car, and office, are these areas calming or do they create feelings of chaos or tension? Clutter is chaotic, and when you are in a cluttered space, you will feel cluttered on the inside.

17. **Consider your friends and relationships**. Do they fulfil you, support your wellbeing, and inspire you to be your best, or do they drag you down?

18. **Make a list of your greatest qualities and read it often**.

19. **Just one thing**. Do one thing that makes you happy every single day. Smell a flower, listen to your favorite song, paint a picture, walk the dog, think of those good things that feed your soul.

20. **Unplug**. Unplug all electronic devices for at least half an hour each day. That means your phone, laptop, tablet, social media, email alerts, landlines, all of it!

21. **Evaluate your social media updates**. Do you really need to be bothered with constant updates from 100 plus people? This type of information overload is really harmful, it promotes stress and prevents your mind from being calm and centred.

22. **Stretch**. One of the easiest and quickest way to destress and recharge is to stretch. *Do it every day*.

23. **Practise positive self-talk**. Use positive affirmations to remind yourself of how great you are and how much you deserve **self-nurture** to promote **self-care** actions.

24. **Spend time in nature**. Nature is soothing, refreshing and re-energises the mind, and spirit.

25. **Journal**. Many people find journaling to be healing, as it allows you vent frustrations, process emotions and reflect.

© Copyright TINA RAE 2023

HANDOUT/ ACTIVITY SHEET

Understanding and **Supporting** **Refugee Children** and **Young People**
A Practical Resource for Teachers, Parents and Carers of Those Exposed to the Trauma of War

Understanding dysregulation and using the 3Rs

Dysregulation occurs when the brain responds to sensory input in a manner that triggers the alarm state.

When a child is dysregulated, it is harder to listen, comprehend and cope.

Remember the 3R's

Regulate: focus on soothing your child. Make them feel calm, safe and loved.

Relate: validate their feelings with your words and tone of voice. "*I know you're upset right now*" "*This is very hard*". Focus on connecting with your child.

Reason: once your child is calm, now it is time to talk about alternatives to behaviour while reinforcing limits you set before. You can reassure them you love them but that the behaviour they're exhibiting is not OK.

Until a child is regulated, they are unlikely to relate to you (*feel connected and comfortable*) and until a child is regulated, they are unlikely to have the mental capacity to reason with you.

REGULATE
RELATE
REASON

© Copyright TINA RAE 2023

S HANDOUT/ ACTIVITY SHEET

Understanding and **Supporting** Refugee Children and Young People
A Practical Resource for Teachers, Parents and Carers of Those Exposed to the Trauma of War

PAGE **139**

Panic attacks
– some helpful reminders

There are many common-sense ways in which we can all assist children

RACING THOUGHTS/FOGGY HEAD
It is just your brain finding threats. These thoughts will probably be untrue and catastrophised and **you are NOT going crazy**.

RAPID BREATHING
Your body's way of increasing oxygen, getting ready to run
– take long, slow, deep breaths down into your belly.

UPSET TUMMY/DIGESTION
Those butterflies are caused by your body redirecting blood flow away from your tummy, into your limbs ready to run. **Its normal** - *drink water and eat some sweets*.

TIGHT THROAT
Muscles tightening from fear responses. **You will not choke**!

SHAKY HANDS
Re-directed blood flow. Hold something to calm you.

RACING HEART
This is your fear response. It is normal and you are not having a heart attack. **Get your doctor to confirm**.

MUSCLE TENSION
From fear response turning on your fight or flight.
Practise muscle relaxation.

© Copyright TINA RAE 2023

PAGE
140

T HANDOUT/
ACTIVITY
SHEET

Understanding
and **Supporting**
Refugee Children
and **Young People**
A Practical Resource for Teachers,
Parents and Carers of Those
Exposed to the Trauma of War

Suicide
INFORMATION SHEET

Suicide is preventable. Young people who are contemplating suicide often give warning signs of their distress. Some signs are subtle, yet some are more common and pronounced. Knowing the risk factors, recognising the warning signs, and knowing how to respond can help prevent suicide.

Suicide Risk Factors

No child is immune to the risk of suicide, **but there are common factors that can increase the chances of having suicidal thoughts.**

- **Previous suicide attempt**(s) *(including a family history of suicide or suicide attempts)*
- **Experiencing crises** *(grief, loss of a family member, friend, or a home, physical or sexual abuse)*
- **Family dysfunction or stress**
- **Chronic bullying**
- **Access to firearms**
- **Mental illness** *(including depression and chronic anxiety)*
- **Substance abuse.**

Having an awareness of any of the risk factors in a child's life is a solid step in the prevention of suicide.

Suicide Warning Signs in Children/Teenagers

The warning signs in children and teens can be subtle but **learning how to spot suicidal tendencies** plays a vital role in intervention.

The most common observable signs are:

- **Talking about wanting to die** *(or drawing out, play-acting/pretending)* **death, suicide, or making plans for suicide**
- **Displaying severe emotional pain or distress**
- **Expressing feelings of hopelessness**
- **Talking about being a burden to others** *(or not belonging in the world/family/ community/school, etc.)*

- **Withdrawing from family, friends, and previously enjoyed activities**
- **Behaviour that is out of character** *(repeated anger, aggressiveness, hostility, or recklessness)*
- **Problems in school** *(poor grades, missed classes, inappropriate behaviour)*
- **Increased risk-taking behaviours** *(vandalism, promiscuous sex, substance abuse).*

A teenager might spout out the alarming words *(especially while agitated, angry, or depressed)*, **"You will be better off without me!", or "What's the point of living?"**, while others remain quiet and internalise their turmoil.

A young child, however, when thinking about what will happen after they are gone, may give their favourite toys and possessions away, or they may talk about splitting the toys up amongst the people that they know. They may also navigate their intense emotions by drawing pictures or writing stories that depict suicide. They may also talk about their feelings of hopelessness, or how they are a burden to others.

We must familiarise ourselves with the common signs of suicide ideation in our young people but know that it can display more subtly in younger children. Regardless of a child's age, however, it is important to never take any warning signs lightly, whether they be subtle or not. **Each child is unique in their own set of circumstances.**

IMPROVE CONNECTEDNESS A child or young person
who is contemplating suicide may not feel able to access the support of those around them. This may be because of fear, perceived rejection, a sense of shame or embarrassment, or because they fear that they may need to share whatever is causing their thoughts of suicide. They may find this difficult to open up about. **It is important** to provide safe spaces and alternative opportunities for schoolchildren to share their story. **It's important** to use language that protects and provides safety and to cultivate an environment where **"nothing is so secret that it can't be shared".**

REDUCE ACCESS TO MEANS It is important to
ensure that the physical environment of your school or college is as safe as possible. The removal of potential ligature points, restricting access to places which facilitate jumping, and removal of harmful substances from public areas, are all examples of how to reduce access to potential means of suicide. **A risk assessment and management strategy may be of value here for your school.**

© Copyright TINA RAE 2023

U HANDOUT/
ACTIVITY
SHEET

Understanding
and Supporting
Refugee Children
and Young People
A Practical Resource for Teachers,
Parents and Carers of Those
Exposed to the Trauma of War

PAGE
141

Positive Remembering

Remembering past events, situations or people with love and affection and in a positive way is a very important way of maintaining wellbeing and good self-esteem. It is particularly useful to develop the ability to transport yourself to positive past times when times get tough or challenging.

- Positive people
- Good times
- Happy moments
- Special events
- Celebrations
- Success
- Achievements
- Loving relationships
- Magic moments
- Special places
- Peaceful moments
- Milestones.

© Copyright TINA RAE 2023

Understanding
and **Supporting**
Refugee Children
and **Young People**
A Practical Resource for Teachers,
Parents and **Carers of Those**
Exposed to the Trauma of War

The power of journaling for wellbeing

We all need to explore and effectively manage our feelings and responses to what happens in our lives on a daily basis. So, why is Journaling so helpful to us? There is a lot of evidence to show us that it has 6 main benefits:

1. It can **improve our mental health** and **wellbeing**
2. It can **help us to record** and **savour special moments**
3. It can **help us to manage or reduce our stress levels**
4. It can **improve our confidence and self-esteem**
5. It can **help us to build our social connections**
6. It can **support us in processing problems and negative feelings or experiences**.

Diaries can help us when we are anxious

When we write about what is happening to us it can sometimes make it easier to make sense of things. If we find we are frequently writing about a particular situation which is making us unhappy, that's a clue that perhaps we need some help. Feelings can be complicated, but writing them down can help us unpick some of the **"knots"**.

Diaries can capture special times and inspire hope when we are feeling down

If you re-read your diaries from when you were smaller you might be reminded about a much-loved family pet, an amazing Christmas or a brilliant holiday. Remembering happy occasions can help us see that life isn't always so bad, and help us feel hopeful about what's to come.

Positive effects are well known

Some of the effects of journaling are well known. Most of us know, for instance, that keeping a Gratitude journal can improve mood. Although versions of this practice differ slightly, the basic idea is to write down a few good things that occur every day for anywhere from 2 to 10 weeks. They can be big things like **"I just got a new job"** or small things we might normally overlook, like **"The flowers in the back garden were beautiful today"**. Given the turmoil in our world, it's easy to overlook the little things that fill us with gratitude, instead focusing exclusively on the many negatives around us. Journaling may be a way of **"hacking into"** the brain, helping us be more mindful of the positive.

Where to start

So, if you're considering a writing practice, how should you begin? Like many things in life, it's a personal choice, and it depends on what you feel would be the most helpful. However, a good place to start might be with a Gratitude journal. Writing about what we're thankful for may not bring about dramatic changes in our lives *but* research consistently shows that it helps. Nobody's pretending that keeping a journal will magically solve the many problems in our world. But during these troubling times, every little bit counts.

© Copyright TINA RAE 2023

W1
HANDOUT/ ACTIVITY SHEET

Understanding and **Supporting** **Refugee Children** and **Young People**
A Practical Resource for Teachers, Parents and Carers of Those Exposed to the Trauma of War

PAGE **143**

Supervision and support
INFORMATION SHEET

A key element of being able to undertake the role of the therapeutic adult supporting refugee children or others who have experienced trauma will be that of accessing appropriate support from colleagues.

Historically, in the field of education, there has been a dearth of such support, particularly in terms of appropriate clinical supervision to staff in schools. However, when you are taking on a role which involves working primarily in a therapeutic way with children and young people, it is essential that you access appropriate supervision from someone who really understands your role, can help you process your own feelings and experiences and ensure that you support young people in an ethical and safe manner.

It is common practice for supervision to be used in counselling, psychotherapy, and other mental health disciplines as well as many other professions engaged in working with both children and adults.

It consists of the practitioner meeting regularly with another professional, not necessarily more senior, but normally with training in the skills of supervision, to discuss casework and other professional issues in a structured way. This is often known as clinical or counselling supervision (*consultation differs in being optional advice from someone without a supervisor's formal authority*). The purpose is to assist the practitioner to reflect upon and learn from his or her experience and progress in expertise, as well as to ensure good service to the client or patient. Learning can then be applied to planning work as well as to diagnostic work and therapeutic work.

Milne (2007) defined clinical supervision as:

"*The formal provision, by approved supervisors, of a relationship-based education and training that is work-focused and which manages, supports, develops and evaluates the work of colleague/s. The main methods that supervisors use are corrective feedback on the supervisee's performance, teaching and collaborative goal-setting. It therefore differs from related activities, such as mentoring and coaching by incorporating an evaluative component. Supervision's objectives are "normative" (e.g. quality control), "restorative" (e.g. encourage emotional processing) and "formative" (e.g. maintaining and facilitating supervisees' competence, capability and general effectiveness)* " p.437.

Some practitioners (*e.g. art, music and drama therapists, chaplains, psychologists, and mental health occupational therapists*) have used this practice for many years. In other disciplines – specifically in education – the practice may not be as evident or so well developed.

The supervision process is interactive *i.e.* a two-way communication based upon trust. This communication may involve the following: solution-focused dialogue leading to well-formed outcomes, active listening, pacing and leading, framing and reframing, problem analysis, non-judgemental challenge, positive by-products, association/disassociation and future pacing.

The idea here is to facilitate thinking rather than be directive *i.e. the Supervisor as a co-constructor in negotiating solutions and a way forward.*

© Copyright TINA RAE 2023

W2 HANDOUT/ ACTIVITY SHEET

Understanding and Supporting Refugee Children and Young People
A Practical Resource for Teachers, Parents and Carers of Those Exposed to the Trauma of War

Supervision and support
INFORMATION SHEET

The following chart illustrates this process in the 4 key areas of setting agenda, identifying the purpose, clarifying the processes involved and outlining the potential outcomes of the supervision process:

It will be helpful to reflect on this process with peers and senior management in a school context to discuss how you may be able to gain this kind of support and benefit in your current role.

AGENDAS/ISSUES

- Individual case work
- Staff team
- Delivery of specific interventions
- Specialist knowledge
- Personal issues *and* emotional aspects
- Practice experiences *e.g.* ethical, moral, organisational, assessment/communication issues
- Achievements.

PURPOSE OF SUPERVISION

- Emotional support
- Affirmation
- Opportunity to reflect
- Integration *and* evaluation of experiences *and* practice in terms of professional judgement, moral *and* ethical standards, personal belief systems *and* attitudes
- Identify strategies *and* problem solve
- Plan *&* target set
- Knowledge *and* skills share *and* development.

PROCESSES

- Building rapport
- Co-construction of agenda
- Sharing of experience *and* knowledge
- Interactive communication
- Solution-focused dialogue
- Active listening
- Pacing – leading
- Framing – reframing
- Non-judgemental challenge
- Facilitation of thinking rather than directive
- Presentation of other perspectives.

OUTCOMES

- Changed state *e.g.* reduction in stress, feeling valued
- New understanding(s) *and* perspective(s)
- New knowledge
- Increased feelings of confidence and competence
- Strategy *and* resource generation
- Sense of belonging, empathy *and* support.

© Copyright TINA RAE 2023

X HANDOUT/ ACTIVITY SHEET

Understanding and Supporting Refugee Children and Young People
A Practical Resource for Teachers, Parents and Carers of Those Exposed to the Trauma of War

PAGE
145

Useful assessments

Anxiety Disorders Interview Schedule for **DSM-IV: Child Version**
Silverman, W.K., & Albano, A.M. *(1996). Manual for the Anxiety Disorders Interview Schedule for DSM-IV: Child Version. USA: Graywind Publications.*

Revised Children's Manifest Anxiety Scale *(RCMAS)*
Reynolds, C.R., & Richmond, B.O. *(1985). Revised Children's Manifest Anxiety Scale. Los Angeles: Western Psychological Service.*

State-Trait Anxiety Inventory for **Children** *(STAIC)*
Spielberger C.D, Gorsuch, R.L., Lushene, R., Vagg, P.R., & Jacobs, G.A. *(1983). Manual for the State-Trait Anxiety Inventory for Children. California: Consulting Psychology Press.*

Social Phobia and **Anxiety Inventory** for **Children** *(SPAIC)*
Beidel, D.C., Turner, S.M., & Morris. T.L. *(1995). A new inventory to assess childhood social anxiety and phobia: The Social Phobia and Anxiety Inventory for children. Psychological Assessment, 7, 73-79.*

Social Anxiety Scale for **Children** *(SCAS)*
La Greca, A.M., Kraslow Dandes. S., Wick, P., Shaw. K., & Stone, W.L. *(1983). Development of the social anxiety scale for children: Reliability and concurrent validity. Journal of Clinical Child Psychology, 17, 84-91.*

Fear Survey Schedule for **Children-Revised** *(FSSC-R)*
Ollendick, T.H. *(1983). Reliability and validity of the revised fear survey schedule for children (FSSCR). Behaviour Research and Therapy, 21, 685-692.*

Multidimensional Anxiety Scale for **Children** *(MASC)*
March, J.S., Parker, J.D.A., Sullivan, K., Stallings, P., & Conners, K. *(1997). The Multidimensional Anxiety Scale for Children (MASC): Factor Structure, Reliability and Validity. Journal of the American Academy of Child and Adolescent Psychiatry, 36, 554-565.*

Screen for the **Child Anxiety Related Emotional Disorders** *(SCARED)*
Birmaher, B., Khetarpal, S., Brent. D., Cully, M., Balach, L., Kaufman. J., & McKenzie Neer. S. *(1997). The Screen for Child Anxiety Related Emotional Disorders (SCARED): Scale Construction and Psychometric Characteristics. Journal of the American Academy of Child and Adolescent Psychiatry, 36, 545-553.*

Child Behavior Checklist *(CBCL)*
Achenbach, T.M., & Edelbrock, C.S. *(1991). Manual for the Child Behavior Checklist and Profile. Burlington: University of Vermont.*

Children's Depression Inventory *(CDI)*
Kovacs, M. *(1981). Ratings scales assess depression in school-aged children. Acta-Paedopsychiatrica, 46, 305-315.*

© Copyright TINA RAE 2023

Y HANDOUT/ ACTIVITY SHEET

Understanding
and Supporting
Refugee Children
and Young People
A Practical Resource for Teachers,
Parents and Carers of Those
Exposed to the Trauma of War

Helpful websites

Action for Children
actionforchildren.org.uk
Charity supporting children, young people and their families across England.

Anxiety UK
03444 775 774 (helpline)
07537 416 905 (text)
anxietyuk.org.uk
Advice and support for people living with anxiety.

Beat
0808 801 0711 (youthline)
0808 801 0811 (studentline)
beateatingdisorders.co.uk
Under 18s helpline, webchat and online support groups for people with eating disorders, such as anorexia and bulimia.

Childline
0800 1111
childline.org.uk
Support for children and young people in the UK, including a free 24-hour helpline.

Hope Again
0808 808 1677
hopeagain.org.uk
Support for young people when someone dies.

Kooth
kooth.com
Counsellors available until 10pm every day. Free, safe and anonymous online counselling for young people.

Mencap
0808 808 1111
mencap.org.uk
Information and advice for people with a learning disability, families and carers.

National Society for the Prevention of Cruelty to Children (NSPCC)
0800 800 5000
0800 1111 (18 or under)
nspcc.org.uk
Support for children and anyone worried about a child.

OCD Youth
ocdyouth.org
Youth Support for young people with obsessive-compulsive disorder (OCD).

On My Mind
annafreud.org/on-my-mind
Information for young people to make informed choices about their mental health and wellbeing.

Samaritans
116 123
samaritans.org
Freepost RSRB-KKBY-CYJK
PO Box 90 90. Stirling FK8 2SA
jo@samaritans.org
24-hour emotional support for anyone who needs to talk.

Refugee council
http://www.refugeecouncil.org.uk/rco_resources

Scottish Refugee council
http://www.scottishrefugeecouncil.org.uk/policy_and_research/information_and_resources

The Mix
0808 808 4994
85258 (crisis messenger service, Text THEMIX)
themix.org.uk
Support and advice for under 25s, including webchat.

UNHCR
http://www.unhcr.org/teaching-about-refugees.html

Welsh Refugee council
http://www.welshrefugeecouncil.org.uk

YoungMinds
0808 802 5544 (parents helpline)
85258 (crisis messenger service, text YM)
youngminds.org.uk
Committed to improving the mental health of babies, children and young people, including support for parents and carers.

References

Banks, **J**. & **Xiaowei**, **X**. *(2020)* The mental health effects of the first two months of lockdown and social distancing during the Covid-19 pandemic in the UK.
Fiscal Studies, 41*(3)*: 685-708.

Barrett, **P**. **M**. & **Turner**, **C**. **M**. *(2001)* Prevention of anxiety symptoms in primary school children: Preliminary results from a universal school-based trial.
British Journal of Clinical Psychology, 40: 399-410.

BPS *(2018)* Guidelines for psychologists working with refugees and asylum seekers in the UK.
Leicester: The British Psychological Society.

Cameron, **R**. & **Maginn**, **C**. *(2008)* The authentic warmth dimension of professional childcare.
British Journal of Social Work, 38*(6)*: 1151-1172.

Chu, **S**. & **Wu**, **H**. *(2012)* Development of effective school-family partnerships for students from culturally and linguistically diverse backgrounds: Special education teachers' and Chinese American parents' perspectives.
Scholarlypartnershipsedu: 6*(1)* 24-37.

Department for Education *(DfE) (2022)* State of the Nation, 2021: Children and young people's wellbeing. Available at:
https://assets.publishing.service.gov.uk/government/uploads/syste m/uploads/attachment_data/file/1053302/State_of_the_Nation_CYP _Wellbeing_2022.pdf *(accessed 28 February 2022)*.

Derluyn, **I**. & **Broekaert**, **E**. *(2007)* Different perspectives on emotional and behavioural problems in unaccompanied refugee children and adolescents.
Ethnicity & Health, 12*(4)*: 141-162.

Ehntholt, **K**. **A**. & **Yule**, **W**. *(2006)* Practitioner review: assessment and treatment of refugee children and adolescents who have experienced war-related trauma.
Journal of Personality and Social Psychology, 47 *(12)*: 1197-210.

Eisenbruch, **M**. *(1991)* From post-traumatic stress disorder to cultural bereavement: Diagnosis of Southeast Asian refugees.
Social Science and Medicine, 33: 673-680.

Fazel, **M**. *(2015)* A moment of change: Facilitating refugee children's mental health in UK schools.
International Journal of Educational Development, 41*(C)*: 255-261.

Geddes, **H**. *(2006)* Attachment in the Classroom.
London: Worth Publishing.

Gerhardt, **S**. *(2004)* Why love matters: How affection shapes the baby's brain.
London: Routledge.

Gottman, **J**. & **Declaire**, **J**. *(1997)* Raising an Emotionally Intelligent Child. The heart of parenting.
New York: Simon and Schuster.

Hanson, **J**. **L**. et al., *(2012)* Structural variations inprefrontal cortex mediate the relationship between early childhood stress and spatial working memory.
Journal of Neuroscience, 32 *(23)*: 7917-7957.

Hope, **J**. *(2011)* New insights into family learning for refugees: Bonding, bridging, and building transcultural capital. Literacy, 45*(2)*: 91-97.

Hughes, **N**. & **Beirens**, **H**. *(2007)* Enhancing educational support: Towards holistic, responsive, and strength-based services for young refugees and asylum-seekers.
Children and Society, 21*(4)*: 261-272.

Kia-Keating, **M**. & **Ellis**, **B**. **H**. *(2007)* Belonging and connection to school in resettlement: Young refugees, school belonging, and psychosocial adjustment.
Clinical Child Psychology and Psychiatry, 12*(1)*: 29-43.

Kim, **S**. **Y**., **Schwartz**, **S**. **J**., **Perreira**, **K**. **M**. & **Juang**, **L**. **P**. *(2018)* Culture's influence on stressors, parental socialization, and developmental processes in the mental health of children of immigrants.
Annual review of clinical psychology, 14: 3 43-370.

Lansford, **J**. **E**., **Dodge**, **K**. **A**., **Pettit**, **G.S.**, **Bates**, **J.E.**, **Crozier**, **J**. & **Kaplow**, **J**. *(2002)*
A 12-year prospective study of the long-term effects of early child physical maltreatment on psychological, behavioral and academic problems in adolescence.
Arch. Pediatr. Adolesc. Med., 156*(8)*: 824-830.

Leung, **B**., **Wu**, **T**., **Questin**, **M**., **Staresnick**, **J**. & **Le**, **P** *(2008)* Communicating with Asian parents and families.
Communiqué, 36*(8)*: insert.

McGloin, **J**. **M**. & **Widom**, **C**. **S**. *(2001)* Resilience among abused and neglected children grown up.
Dev. Psychopathology, 13*(4)*: 1021-1038.

McMullen, **J**. **D**., **O'Callaghan**, **P**., **Richards**, **J**., **Eakin**, **J**. & **Rafferty**, **H**. *(2012)* Screening for Traumatic Exposure and Psychological Distress among War-Affected Adolescents in PostConflict northern Uganda.
Social Psychiatry and Psychiatric Epidemiology, 47*(9)*: 1489-1498.

McMullen, **J**. **D**, **Jones**, **S**., **Campbell**, **R**., **McLaughlin**, **J**., **McDade**, **B**., **O'Lynn**, **P**. & **Glen**, **C**. *(2020)* Sitting on a wobbly chair: mental health and wellbeing among newcomer pupils in Northern Irish schools.
Emotional and Behavioural Difficulties, 25*(2)*: , 125-138.

Milne, **D**. *(2007)* An empirical definition of clinical supervision.
British Journal of Clinical Psychology, 46: 437-447.

Miller, **J**. **P**., **Rosengren**, **K**. **S**., & **Gutiernez**, **I**. **T**. *(2014)* Children's understanding of death: Towards a contextualized and integrated account.
Monographs of the Society for Research in Child Development, Vol 79*(1)* :1-18.

PAGE
148

Understanding and **Supporting**
Refugee Children and Young People:
A Practical Resource for Teachers, Parents and
Carers of Those Exposed to the Trauma of War

References

Moore, G. & **Morgan**, K. *(2021)* Healthy futures for young people.
Schools Health Research Network:
Cardiff University. [AK1] www.shrn.org.uk (accessed 28th February 2022).

Palmer, J. & **Edward**, C. D. *(2001)*
Fifty modern thinkers on education.
London: Routledge.

Pearlman, L. A., & **Maclan**, P. S. *(1994)* Vicarious traumatization: An
empirical study of the effects of trauma work on trauma therapists.
Professional Psychology: Research and Practice, *26(6)*: 558-565.

Perry, B. *(1994)* Neurobiological sequelae of childhood trauma: Post-
traumatic stress disorders in children, In M. **Murberg** *(Ed.)*,
Catecholamines in post-traumatic stress disorder emerging
concepts *(pp. 253-276)*.
Washington, DC: American Psychiatric Press.

Perry, B. *(2002)* Plasticity, Memory and Cortical Modulation in the Brain
http://www.childtraumaacademy.com/amazing_brain/lesson05/page02.html

Perry, B. & **Hambrick**, E. *(2008)* The neurosequential model of
therapeutics.
Reclaiming Children and Youth, *17(3)*: 38-43.

Perry, B. D. *(2007)* Stress, Trauma and post-traumatic stress
disorders in children. An Introduction.
The Child Trauma Academy.

Peterson, C., **Maier**, S. F. & **Seligman**, M. E. P. *(1995)*
Learned Helplessness: A Theory for the Age of Personal Control.
New York: Oxford University Press.

Rae, T., **Walshe**, J. & **Wood**, J. *(2017)* The Essential Guide to Using
Mindfulness with Young People.
Buckingham: Hinton House Publishers.

Rae, T. *(2020)* A Toolbox of Wellbeing Helpful Strategies and
Activities for Children, Teens, Their Carers, and Teachers.
Buckingham: Hinton House Publishers.

Reed, R. V., **Fazel**, M., **Jones**, L., **Panter-Brick**, C. & **Stein**, A. *(2012)*
Mental health of displaced and refugee children resettled in low-
income and middle-income countries: Risk and protective factors.
Lancet, *379(9812)*: 250-65.

Rock, D. et al., *(2012)* The healthy mind platter.
Neuro Leadership Journal *(Issue 4)*.

Roy, L. A. & **Roxas**, K. C. *(2011)* Whose deficit is this anyhow?
Exploring counter-stories of Somali Bantu refugees' experiences in
"doing school."
Harvard Educational Review, *81(3)*: 521-541.

Rutter, M. *(2006)* Implications of resilience concepts for scientific
understanding.
Annals of the New York Academy of Science, 1094: 1-12.

Saakvitne, K. W., **Gamble**,
S., **Pearlman**, L. & **Lev**, B.
(2000)
Risking connection: A
training curriculum for
working with survivors of
childhood abuse.
Lutherville, MD: Sidran Press.

Saakvitne, K. W., **Gamble**, S., **Pearlman**, L.
A. & **the Staff of the Traumatic Stress Institute** *(1996)*
Transforming the pain: A workbook on vicarious traumatization.
New York: W.W. Norton.

Srinivasa Murthy, R., & **Lakshminarayana**, R. *(2006)* Mental
health consequences of war: A brief review of research findings.
World Psychiatry, *5(1)*: 25-30.

Sroufe, A., **Egeland**, B., **Carlson**, E. & **Collins**, A. *(2005)*
The Development of the Person: The Minnesota study of risk and
adaptation from birth to adulthood.
New York: Guildford Press.

Taylor, S. & **Sidhu**, R. K. *(2012)* Supporting refugee students in
schools: what constitutes inclusive education?
International Journal of Inclusive Education, *16(1)*: 39-56.

Teicher, M., **Andersen**, S., **Polcari**, A., **Anderson**, C., **Navalta**, C.
& **Kim**, D. *(2003)* The neurobiological consequences of early stress
and childhood maltreatment.
Neuroscience and Biobehavioral Reviews, *27(1-2)*: 33-44.

Thambirajah, M. S., **Grandison**, K. J. & **De-Hayes**, L. *(2008)*
Understanding school refusal: a handbook for professionals in
education, Health and Social Care.
London: UKL Jessica Kingsley.

Torre, J.B. & **Lieberman**, M.D. *(2018)*. Putting feelings into words:
Affect labeling as Implicit emotion regulation.
Emotion Review, *10(2)*: 116-124.

Turney, K. & **Kao**, G. *(2009)* Barriers to school involvement: Are
immigrant parents disadvantaged?
Journal of Educational Research, *102(4)*: 257-271.

van der Kolk, B. A., **Greenberg**, M. S., **Orr**, S. & **Pittman**, R. K.
(1989) Pain Perception and endogenous opioids in post traumatic
stress disorder.
Psychopharm Bull, 25: 117-121.

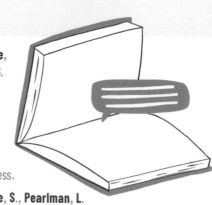

Index

PAGE
150

Understanding and Supporting
Refugee Children and Young People:
A Practical Resource for Teachers, Parents and Carers of Those Exposed to the Trauma of War

Index

Index

Understanding and Supporting
Refugee Children and Young People:
A Practical Resource for Teachers, Parents and Carers of Those Exposed to the Trauma of War

Index